1991

Moral Issues in Military
Decision Making

Moral Issues in Military Decision Making

Anthony E. Hartle

University Press of Kansas

Published by the University Press of Kansas (Lawrence, Kansas
66045), which was organized by the Kansas Board of Regents and is
operated and funded by Emporia State University, Fort Hays State
University, Kansas State University, Pittsburg State University,
the University of Kansas, and Wichita State University

Library of Congress Cataloging-in-Publication Data

Hartle, Anthony E., 1942–
    Moral issues in military decision making.
    Bibliography: p.
    Includes index.
    1. Military ethics. I. Title.
U22.H38   1989   172'.42   88-33918
ISBN 0-7006-0397-2 (alk. paper)

British Library Cataloguing in Publication Data is available.

Printed in the United States of America
10 9 8 7 6 5 4 3 2

Contents

Acknowledgments

Friends who fell in battle in a strange war far from American shores provided the impetus for this endeavor—leaders who marched steadily forward despite the doubts and the shadows to give the last full measure of service to their nation: Kirby Wilcox, Michael Nawrosky, Clair Thurston, H. P. Kindleberger. They were joined by many others. As I later sifted through the philosophical wisdom of our culture, trying to make sense of my generation's experience, I was particularly grateful for the assistance of Robert L. Causey, Paul Woodruff, Grayson D. Browning, and Edward Sherman, each of whom contributed to my understanding of the subjects I discuss in this text and encouraged me to seek publication.

I thank Cambridge University Press for permission to use copyrighted material from my article, "Humanitarianism and the Laws of War," which was published in *Philosophy* 61 (1986). Portions of that article appear in chapter 5.

Chapter One

Introduction:
The Hardest Place

For war is the hardest place: if comprehensive and consistent moral judgments are possible there, they are possible everywhere.[1]
— *Michael Walzer*

The environment in which members of the military must operate poses a severe threat to consistent moral behavior. In addition to the inevitable stresses of leadership in the profession of arms, men and women in uniform today face a confusing variety of inconsistencies in national policy and government practice.[2] The United States engages in an international arms race that threatens humanity as a whole; the government adheres to a strategic nuclear policy that seeks to avoid nuclear war by threatening the indiscriminate slaughter of millions of people. The state that is defended by the military professional champions the cause of peace while supporting protracted military involvements abroad and providing massive quantities of arms to potential belligerents around the world. Defense of American values constitutes the soldier's fundamental purpose, but members of the government of the state that embodies those values frequently deem it necessary to operate pragmatically rather than on the basis of principle.

In such an environment, confusion multiplies rapidly. Thus, for practical reasons alone, the professional military ethic becomes a matter of particular concern. The ethic needs to be a workable guide that cuts through such confusion and illuminates the standards applied to moral decisions. Confusion hinders effectiveness, and how effectively the military services perform their primary function — the systematic application of force — can have momentous consequences for the state they serve.

1

For the American military, the professional military ethic is also a concern for an additional reason: members of our armed forces make a moral commitment through their commissioning or enlistment oath. They make a commitment to a set of values, which provides a depth and complexity to the ethic that require more than a superficial examination if the ethic is to be understood and properly applied. A group of soldiers could make a commitment to defend a certain piece of ground, for example, and such a commitment might well be construed as a choice involving a distinct moral obligation on their part. Considerable conceptual complexity is added, however, if a group makes a moral commitment to adhere to and support a set of values that itself has extensive moral implications. Such a situation exists when new members of the military swear to "support and defend the Constitution" against all enemies.

My discussion will examine the complexity of the existing American professional military ethic (PME) and the justification for it. I hope to clarify the moral framework within which moral decisions must be made, both in time of peace, when such decisions are often quite difficult, and in time of war, which is indeed "the hardest place."

The nature of that place eludes accurate description in ordered prose on a written page, but the testimony of those who endure war nonetheless suggests the savage quandaries that inevitably arise. James McDonough relates a typically trying situation he encountered as a young lieutenant in the Vietnam War. With part of his platoon, he rushed to the assistance of a stay-behind ambush that had initiated a firefight. In the action, one of the members of the ambush element had been seriously wounded and needed medical help, but at the base of the hill on which he was located, Lieutenant McDonough encountered a minefield that effectively blocked him from moving to the assistance of the stay-behind group. Desperately casting about for a way to proceed, he discovered a frightened local farmer cowering nearby. Through his interpreter, McDonough demanded that the farmer show them how to get through the minefield, only to be refused.

> "Ask him again, Nhan," I ordered.
> Again the farmer refused, his eyes widening in fear. I took out my knife. "Nhan, tell him I'll kill him right now if he doesn't tell us."
> I had crossed the line. I wouldn't have killed him, but he

didn't know that, and the threat itself was criminal. But I weighed that against the bleeding soldier and the others who might bleed if we didn't get through to them quickly. A leader has no one to look to for advice on such decisions. He must do what he thinks is best, but he must not fool himself as to the consequences of his choice. War is not a series of case studies that can be scrutinized with objectivity. It is a series of stark confrontations that must be faced under the most emotion-wrenching conditions. War is the suffering and death of people you know, set against a background of the suffering and death of people you do not.[3]

Lieutenant McDonough reached the group under fire and evacuated the wounded man, whose life was saved by the action. Does that justify his treatment of the farmer? In some instances, can we justifiably violate the laws of war in order to achieve specific ends? If so, how can we identify such circumstances? Such situations, repeated with terrible frequency, corrode the soul and warp moral sensibilities.

On a more massive wartime scale, the responsibility of deciding who is to live seems more than should be asked of any conscientious person. Gen. Omar Bradley faced such a decision at St. Lô during World War II, when the fate of millions hung in the balance. That situation, suggestive of the kind of dilemma likely to be common in future major conflicts, further illustrates why the maelstrom of war becomes the hardest place.

In July 1944, American forces were poised for what General Bradley called "the most decisive battle of our war in Europe."[4] After three weeks of being bottled up in Normandy after the invasion, Allied forces were committed to a major breakthrough in the area of St. Lô, where armored forces would be able to operate on solid ground beyond the hedgerows. Michael Walzer has pointed out one difficult moral aspect of that operation that illustrates the severe stress on conscience which can be created by military decisions.[5] Part of the plan for the breakout, dubbed Operation COBRA, was a relatively new concept called carpet bombing. At the point of attack in the enemy lines, an area of five square miles was to be pulverized with bombs by an overwhelming force of 350 fighter planes and 1,500 heavy bombers. The infantry units would then secure the penetration to allow a breakthrough by armored elements.

When General Bradley briefed a group of journalists, however, just before the battle was to begin, one asked about the French citizens of St. Lô, who would be subjected to the Allied bombs along with the Germans. Would they be warned somehow? General Bradley, having already wrestled with that question, painfully shook his head, "as if to escape the necessity for saying no."[6] Warning the civilians would jeopardize the operation, and the stakes were too high.

But the fate of French civilians was not the only morally agonizing issue in this offensive. An important part of Bradley's plan was to use a road running parallel to the American front as a guide for the huge air armada that would launch COBRA. The major artery, clearly visible from the air, would allow the bombing to proceed with a reasonable degree of security for the infantry units in attack positions. Bombers were seldom used in support of ground operations because they were notoriously inaccurate; much too often bombs landed on friendly troops rather than on the enemy. On 23 July the long chains of aircraft were launched from airfields in England, only to be turned back by a heavy cloud cover that necessitated postponing the attack twenty-four hours. One group of bombers, however, flew on to the target and dropped their bombs—on the U.S. Thirtieth Infantry Division, one of the assault units. When Bradley investigated, he found that the bombers had approached over the heads of friendly troops, perpendicular to the front rather than parallel to it. That approach made error by the bombardiers much more likely.

After a lengthy, frustrating series of indirect communications, General Bradley's headquarters found that the air forces indeed had decided to use a perpendicular approach to the front, despite the general's firm insistence during the planning phase on the parallel course. The lone group of bombers had not been mistaken in its route. General Bradley then had to make yet another dispiriting moral decision in COBRA. Changing the approach of the long parade of bombers, timed almost to the second as aircraft taking off from dozens of airfields were consolidated into one striking arm, meant further postponement, which could have made the plan of attack evident to the Germans. Proceeding with COBRA meant almost certain U.S. casualties. General Bradley decided the attack must begin on schedule.

After considerable difficulty, the breakout succeeded in spectacular fashion, launching Patton's Third Army on its famous race across Europe. The early hours of the offensive were particularly difficult, however, for the COBRA bombers did hit American units in attack positions. The misguided bombs severely pounded the Ninth and Thirtieth divisions, resulting in several hundred dead and wounded. One of the dead was Lt. Gen. Lesley J. McNair, considered one of our great combat leaders. General Bradley was probably fortunate that the press of combat allowed little time to dwell on the burdens of conscience that are unavoidable for those in command.

Profound moral questions are at issue in the complex decisions necessitated by war, but views concerning the status of morality differ widely. Some consider morality mere social convention; some view it as no more than a system of persuasion; others argue for moral absolutes to which everyone should conform. But all recognize it as a factor that regulates social behavior. If morality is to operate in that function, it should be as free from internal contradiction as possible. Commitment to values and moral principles provides reasons for acting. Consistent, effective action will follow only from a coherent set of principles of action and rules for conduct, while general moral principles will provide the foundation for specific guides for action. The consistency with which we follow such guides, then, will necessarily be a function of the coherence of and justification for the general principles. Accordingly, my examination of the American professional military ethic will concern its content, its coherence, and its rational justifiability.

In my discussion of these aspects of the PME, I examine the claim that the military role is what sociologists sometimes refer to as a "differentiated role." Various writers, among them Alan Goldman, Richard Wasserstrom, and Robert Veatch, have been concerned with the special norms of professional groups in terms of role-differentiated behavior. Under this concept, we classify roles on the basis of the degree to which various considerations that otherwise would be relevant or even decisive in moral evaluations are disregarded or weighed less heavily.[7]

The profession of law, an important part of our legal system, recognizes the *Code of Professional Responsibility* established by the American Bar Association. The code articulates the professional ethic and establishes the differentiated rules (some of which also have legal force) that most state codes incorporate. Under that code, one provision requires lawyers to give every client their best efforts in furthering the client's interests. Sometimes those interests are immoral, but so long as they are legal, the professional code enjoins lawyers to do their best to realize those interests. That is one sense in which we say that lawyers' roles are differentiated—meaning that the moral guidance for lawyers in their professional roles may call for actions which are different from those appropriate for a general member of society. Rules that specify different actions for lawyers are said to be justified because the service provided to members of society in general is so critical that certain apparent violations of society's moral rules for conduct are justified if they are necessary to maintain the institution of law. That is, the role-differentiated behavior of lawyers finds justification in the claim that such behavior is necessary to realize the fundamental values of society. Thus, the fundamental values that generate moral rules requiring general members of society to act one way in normal day-to-day life might call for lawyers to act quite differently in their professional roles.[8] Understanding that the profession of arms has a similar role-differentiated character can help to clarify the moral nature of the professional military ethic.

A particular case that occurred in 1973 manifests the concept of differentiation.[9] A mechanic from Syracuse, New York, killed four people who were camping in the Adirondacks. He apparently chose his victims at random. During the next month, authorities captured the murderer, Robert Garrow, and indicted him for the murder of one of the four, a college student. Police had recovered one additional body, but at the time of Garrow's arrest, two of the victims were not even known to be dead. One of those was a young Illinois woman, the other a teenage runaway. The court appointed two lawyers to defend Garrow, who told them of raping and killing the Illinois woman and subsequently hiding her body in a mine shaft. The lawyers investigated and found the body, but left it and did not report their discovery. About a month later, following Garrow's instructions, they found the second body, which they also did not report.

The father of the Illinois woman, learning that the lawyers were defending a man accused of killing a camper in the Adirondacks, traveled to Syracuse and asked the lawyers if they had any information that might shed light on the whereabouts of his missing daughter. They said no. Later, in court testimony, Garrow implicated himself in the other three murders. Amid general outrage, the lawyers explained that because their knowledge of the other murders and the location of the bodies was privileged information received from their client, their professional ethical code prohibited revealing the facts. And however cruel and unfeeling that choice may seem, the lawyer-client privilege is one of the foundational principles of our adversary legal system, in which both defense lawyers and prosecutors present the strongest cases possible. The assumption is that justice will best be served when that happens. If clients cannot be completely honest with their lawyers and be assured that the communication will go no further, the lawyers cannot present the most effective defense. The lawyers in the Garrow case followed this rule: "Lawyers should never reveal information gained in the confidential lawyer-client relationship, unless the information is necessary to prevent a crime or to save a life."[10]

The Garrow case illustrates that the moral rules lawyers must follow are exactly the same as those members of the general population must follow, unless different standards are justified by the benefit that society would receive by adherence to differentiated rules. Because society benefits enormously from a stable and consistent legal system that incorporates fundamental values, our society considers that the differentiated rules necessary to maintain such a system are justified. At least, that is the theory. And from this view, lawyers are said to have a differentiated role in society.

With that model in mind, I want to ask whether the role of the military officer is indeed a differentiated role, and how we might justify the professional military ethic that exists.

Society grants to members of the military possession and control of an elaborate array of weaponry—weapons of great power forbidden to general members of society. In addition, military leaders have the authority to order other persons into situations of great danger, sometimes when death is likely. And, of course, soldiers are authorized to use deadly force in ways that general members of the society are not. These factors suggest a differentiated role for the military.

Society benefits in a straightforward sense. The world of nations in some ways resembles Thomas Hobbes' state of nature, in which every individual seeks his own interest and must guard against all others. No higher authority exists—at least, to acknowledge the United Nations, no effective one—to provide protection or to enforce justice. The simple fact is that we must have competent military forces if we are to maintain our way of life. The military services exist to protect the state with armed force as necessary.

The needs of society appear to justify the existence of the military profession, then, just as the needs of society support the existence of the legal profession. And the military has a professional code governing the conduct of its members, just as the legal and medical professions do. The military code in the United States, however, is not a formally codified set of rules.[11] The product of tradition and experience, it can be explained in terms of three primary influences.

The three factors that have shaped the American professional military ethic are the functional requirements of military service, the international laws of war, and the core values of American society. In the pages ahead we will examine the relationship among these primary influences and how the PME they produce is applied. In doing so, we will explore each of the factors as well as some of the institutional characteristics of the military profession. We will also have to consider just what constitutes the American PME.

Chapter Two

The Military as a Profession

The Nature of Professions

What characteristics identify a particular activity as a profession? Alan Goldman, in *The Moral Foundations of Professional Ethics*, says that "we may take it as definitional of professions that they involve the application of a specialized body of knowledge in the service of important interests of a clientele."[1] This appears to be a necessary condition, though a gangland "hit man" might qualify as a professional if we accept this definition as complete. So would harbormasters and Alaskan hunting guides, which suggests that some additional discriminating characteristics are necessary. Even so, I contend that under any of the authoritative definitions available, a distinct segment of the armed forces clearly qualifies as a professional group.[2] The officer corps constitutes that group. In addition, the senior noncommissioned officer corps meets most requirements. Needless to say, the sense of the term "profession" that I cite refers to an occupation involving advanced study and specialization, not one that includes activity in which skill is rewarded by money in contrast to amateur or volunteer activity; e.g., hockey players in the National Hockey League and professional artists, among others.

Huntington's View

Samuel Huntington, despite his difficulties with the National Academy of Sciences, is an authority on the sociology of professions. He has identified three characteristics as necessary for any activity to achieve the status of a profession: expertise, corporateness, and

9

responsibility.[3] Huntington contends that career military service possesses all three characteristics and concludes the following:

> The modern officer corps is a highly professional body. It has its own expertise, corporateness, and responsibility. The existence of this profession tends to imply, and the practice of the profession tends to engender among its members, a distinctive outlook on international politics, the role of the state, the place of force and violence in human affairs, the nature of man and society, and the relationship of the military profession to the state.[4]

Huntington's "expertise" involves the satisfaction of a significant social need, which provides one argument for the justification of the profession's ethic (a subject I touched upon in the Introduction and to which I will return in chapter 6). Medicine, for example, concerns the need to preserve human life and to minimize suffering. One gains professional expertise through a lengthy period of formal education. "Professional knowledge . . . is intellectual and capable of preservation in writing."[5] Usually, the profession itself controls and perpetuates professional education through its own facilities.

A particular profession sees itself as a corporate body distinct from laymen as a result of its expertise and the nature of its activity. The profession generates and adheres to its own criterion of competence, and it normally controls admission to its ranks. Most activities recognized as professions enforce the standards of performance by this means and may also terminate membership when the standards are not maintained. The authority to police its own ranks is one of the distinctive characteristics of a profession.

The sense of corporateness results partially from the social responsibility borne by the profession. The expertise is one deemed critical, or at least necessary in some sense, by society. The professional gains special status and in return is expected to recognize a social obligation to provide a special expertise, so that commitment to the role entails a "profession" of obligation to society. The nature and substance of the obligation are normally articulated through a written code governing conduct—a statement of the professional ethic—which establishes standards for behavior within the profession. One of various functions served by the code is that of safeguard-

ing the relevant interests of society, which is of particular interest
with respect to justifying the ethic. (That is not to deny, of course,
that the ethic of a profession may serve the personal interests of members of the profession. It often does.) In some situations, the benefits
to society can be realized only if the professional operates under special norms,[6] or so it is claimed; those cases concern us here.

Expertise

Huntington argues persuasively that the military institution has
the three characteristics — expertise, corporateness, and social responsibility — to qualify it as a profession. He points out that the members
of most professions have a diversified basic education supplemented
by a formal, substantial period of advanced education that qualifies
them in their occupation. The profession of arms indeed exemplifies
this pattern. Military officers begin with a bachelor's degree (or complete one shortly after commissioning) and then progress through a
series of military schools at different points in their careers if they
remain on active duty. Those in leadership positions in the services
go through a program of education that typically extends over a period of twenty years.

In the army system of professional education, junior officers complete a basic course which teaches fundamental skills and small unit
tactics. After several years of professional experience, officers attend a
year-long course tailored to the officer's branch of service — infantry,
artillery, signal corps, and so on. All army officers must attend a two-
month staff course; later, selected field-grade officers (about 50 per-
cent of the total number eligible for consideration) spend a year at
the Command and General Staff College. Finally, after sixteen to
twenty years of service, officers selected on the basis of merit attend
the Army War College, where the curriculum concentrates on strategy and international relations. At some point, most officers also
receive an advanced degree from a civilian institution at the direction of the army. The other military services pursue programs of professional development similar in nature.

The extensive educational programs of the armed forces focus on
the unique character of military service and the peculiar sphere of military competence: the systematic application of force for political purposes. An effective commander of an army division must have a high

degree of competence that requires extensive training, wide experience, and special abilities. The same is obviously true of the captain of an aircraft carrier or a group of ships in the navy. An understanding of the relationship between tactical alternatives and organizational capabilities is essential to competent performance, as is a comprehensive knowledge of the technological aspects of training for and conducting combat operations. Leaders in all the services must develop the interpersonal skills that allow them to motivate and to command others. The direction of complex staff procedures and the command of large numbers of men in the stress of battle require capabilities normally achieved only after years of dedicated application and thorough study. One detailed analysis of command identifies four "learning objectives" for military leaders:

1. Knowledge. Information, data, facts, theories, concepts [includes military tactics, weapons capabilities, and logistical requirements].
2. Skills. Abilities that can be developed and manifested in performance, not merely in potential. . . . Includes technical, communications, information-retrieval, and some analytical skills.
3. Insights. Ideas and thoughts derived internally from an ability to see and understand clearly the nature of things. Necessary part of making judgments, of deciding, of "putting it all together," of "being aware" of wisdom, far-sightedness. . . . Cannot be taught directly, but can be induced by qualified teachers. Generally a product of education [and long experience] rather than training.
4. Values. Convictions, fundamental beliefs, standards governing the behavior of people. Includes attitudes towards professional standards such as duty, integrity, loyalty, patriotism, public service, and phrases such as "take care of your people" and "accomplish your missions." . . . Values, like insights, must be derived by the individual, if they are to have meaning.[7]

Thus, to be prepared for his responsibilities, a commander must be proficient in a variety of areas. He must be a "tactician, strategist, warrior, ethicist, leader, manager, and technician."[8] Another long-time student of the military profession notes that as a strategist alone, a soldier must be prepared for the following tasks:

1. Understand and support political *goals*, to insure effective coordination of policy and strategy.

2. Select military *objectives* that will lead logically to the achievement of political aims.
3. Allocate military *resources* and establish correct priorities.
4. Conduct war in a way that sustains *support* of the home front.
5. Maintain a proportional *balance* between the application of violence and the value of the political goals.[9]

A professional soldier prepared for high command is necessarily a person of unusual expertise, one who has been carefully selected and in whom the country has made a major investment.

At the turn of the century, during the Boer War in South Africa, a situation developed that provides a telling insight into the responsibilities of a military commander.[10] The case emphasizes both the strategic aspects noted in the previous list and the issue of moral responsibility that will concern us in the chapters ahead.

In South Africa, Britain faced a particularly unpleasant war against the Boers. The rapid defeat of the Boers had not come about as expected, so to hasten the event Britain placed in command its most distinguished soldier, the hero of Khartoum, Lord Kitchener. He was determined to bring the war to a rapid and successful conclusion, but he found some daunting obstacles. Many heads of Boer households and the able-bodied men of the Boer families had left home to join the Boer commandos, leaving behind the wives, children, and the infirm. Those remaining on the farms, where the rugged pioneers faced daily hardship in normal times, suffered greatly as the war dragged on. Perhaps of even more concern to Lord Kitchener was the fact that they also provided logistical support and intelligence to the Boer fighters. Kitchener ordered all the families removed from the farms and placed in great concentration camps, the infamous *laagers*, both to provide protection for the noncombatants and to further Britain's war effort. Unfortunately, the British had failed to make adequate provisions for medical care, administration, or even food in the camps. Whether adequate care was even possible in view of the constrained resources and the ongoing war effort is uncertain, but in the months that followed, over twenty thousand Boer women and children died.

The brutal conditions in the camps were widely reported in British papers, and many people in England came to question the war and the actions of the British forces (a development that has a painfully familiar ring), making prosecution of the war much more difficult for the British government. Kitchener had made what he believed was a logical military decision in wartime, but he had failed to give adequate consideration to the logistical and the concomitant moral dimensions of his decision. The results of establishing the concentration camps affected the achievement of political goals and changed the strategic situation. Kitchener obviously did not sustain the support of the home front. The disastrous results also illustrate the issue of a professional soldier's social responsibility.

Social Responsibility

The abilities of a professional officer corps are essential to the security of national interests in a world of shrinking resources and ideologically competitive states. That, at least, is the clear consensus of the American people, whose elected representatives have created and maintained the authorization for such an organization. That a strong and capable military force is considered essential to national interests seems undeniable if one considers the huge budgetary appropriations for defense expenditures. As we have seen in recent years, any failure of the military is viewed with considerable alarm accompanied by demands for more effective training and improved leadership. Despite wishes to the contrary, the prevailing view in Western society seems to be that the use of force is an inherent aspect of the human condition.

The history of this century certainly supports such a view. In 1987, over twenty wars—under the narrowest definition—were under way around the world. Using a broad definition, we could have counted over one hundred. By one estimate, armed conflicts have cost at least sixteen million lives since the end of World War II.[11] Modern society, curiously, does not seem greatly alarmed by the fact that people around the world face a much greater likelihood of destruction from conventional warfare than they do from the looming threat of a nuclear holocaust.[12] An external observer of world affairs might well conclude that we have accepted the inevitability of armed conflict in world affairs.

The likelihood of armed conflict strongly suggests that military forces are essential to the defense of national interests. Nonetheless, historically, a powerful military has also been a distinct threat to representative government. The problems of the Aquino administration in the Philippines and the struggles of Latin American countries provide recent examples. American society since the Revolutionary War has manifested an antipathy toward the concept of a standing army and has traditionally harbored a deep-seated distrust of military professionals. As a result, with very few exceptions, civil-military relations have been stable and unambiguous. In general, American military forces and military leaders have always been an obedient arm of the state and strictly subordinate to civilian authority. The military, reflecting the attitude of American society, has placed particular emphasis on the concept of social responsibility—the idea that professional officers must use their expertise only for society's benefit. More importantly, the measures necessary to achieve that benefit are determined by the civilian authority. These observations support Huntington's contention that a particularly strong sense of social responsibility characterizes the profession of arms in the United States.

Military professionals must also be competent to perform their duties. That obligation constitutes another facet of their social responsibility. The criticality of their role as the ultimate bulwark of society, called upon to protect the nation, makes competence a moral imperative.[13] Here again, the parallel with other professions such as medicine and engineering seems obvious. The disastrous effects of incompetence generate continuous concern within the profession about individual skills and performance. The military's complex systems of schooling and individual evaluation, both of which continue throughout every soldier's career, reflect that concern.

Corporateness

Few will question the argument for the corporateness of the military leadership. The officer corps itself evaluates and judges the conduct and competence of individual officers (to include noncommissioned officers). Huntington accurately describes the corporate nature of the organization in these words: .

> The functional imperatives give rise to complex vocational institutions which mold the officer corps into an autonomous social unit. Entrance into this unit is restricted to those with the requisite education and training and is usually permitted only at the lowest level of professional competence. The cor-

porate structure of the officer corps includes not just the official bureaucracy but also societies, associations, schools, journals, customs, and traditions. The professional world of the officer tends to encompass an unusually high proportion of his activities. He normally lives and works apart from the rest of society; physically and socially he probably has fewer nonprofessional contacts than most other professional men. The line between him and the layman or civilian is publicly symbolized by uniforms and insignia of rank.[14]

The foregoing, in brief, presents Huntington's argument for the claim that military career officers are members of a profession. But just who fits into the category of the military professional is not as clear as it might seem. Are naval ensigns professionals? Marine Corps master sergeants? career Chemical Corps officers?

The military services have become highly complex organizations. The functions and traditions of the air force, the army, the navy, and the Coast Guard vary widely. Within each of these major divisions of the military, the vast majority of soldiers, sailors, marines, and airmen are in the lower ranks and are not clear-cut professionals under the qualifying characteristics given above, primarily because they do not acquire and apply a significant body of theoretical knowledge and they lack any organization exhibiting self-direction and self-regulation. The particular corporate character of the officer corps is emphasized by a distinctive evaluation system, different from that of the enlisted ranks, and by the special authority and responsibilities noted in the commission and the oath of office. The senior noncommissioned officers of the services, however, show strong attributes of professionalism. To further complicate the picture, among the officers of the services are numerous supporting specialists, many of them professionals in other areas. Included are doctors, lawyers, veterinarians, finance experts, and a host of others necessary for the support and maintenance of a large, modern military force. A practical distinction thus exists between the purely military professional and the supporting cast that provides services not wholly peculiar to the military.

So the lines demarcating the professional component of the military services are difficult to fix. Actually, a spectrum exists. To the degree that various rank levels and positions in the military possess those characteristics sufficient for classification as "professional," they should be considered professionalized. In general terms, the following appears to be true:

> There is no absolute difference between professional and other kinds of occupational behavior, but only relative differences with respect to certain attributes common to all occupational behavior. . . . [On this view] the medical profession is more professional than the nursing profession, and the medical doctor who does university research is more professional than the medical doctor who provides minor medical services in a steel plant. Professionalism is a matter of degree.[15]

I will focus on the officer corps, by and large, because it possesses to the greatest degree the characteristics usually cited for a profession. Officers constitute a clearly defined group, though obviously not all officers are professionals with respect to expertise and career commitment.[16] Officers comprise the most critical group in terms of decision-making responsibility, and the military ethic applies most forcefully and significantly to them.

Another perspective that also suggests a focus on the officer corps is that of noblesse oblige.[17] The term refers to the obligations to act honorably that come with a conferred station. Under this view, the more power and authority conferred by a societal role, the more stringent are the moral requirements of the role. Because power corrupts, society's demands for moral conduct and character increase as the importance of the position increases. The principle is not a new one, as John Adams' comment concerning the public's "right to know" indicates: "They have a right, an indisputable, inalienable, indefeasible, divine right to that most dreaded and envied kind of knowledge — I mean, of the characters and conduct of their rulers."[18]

In the military sphere, the concept of noblesse oblige has nowhere been captured more dramatically than by the Israeli war hero, Nahum Arieli, who commanded an isolated unit on a critically important hill during the early struggle for Israeli independence. When the unit was overrun by a much larger Arab force, he ordered a retreat. To have any chance of success, however, the retreat had to be protected by covering fire, which meant a portion of the unit had to remain in position as the retreat commenced. The Israeli commander issued an order that has come to represent the ethos of the Israeli officer corps: "All enlisted men are to withdraw; the officers will cover the retreat." Only one officer survived.[19]

The concept that officers must meet higher moral requirements also supports my focus on the moral obligations of the officer corps. Here is where we will find the essence of military professionalism.

Other Views of Professionalism

The sociological approach to professionalism is one that views a profession as an organized group that is constantly interacting with the society that forms its matrix, which performs its social functions through a network of formal and informal relationships, and which creates its own subculture requiring adjustments to it as a prerequisite for career success.[20]

—Ernest Greenwood

This rather technical definition certainly fits the military, for of all groups in society it is one of the most obviously organized elements. Interaction with society occurs constantly, from recruiting programs to the reality of the military-industrial complex. The military performs its social function through a prescribed set of formal relationships and a vast, intricate set of informal relationships involving both governmental leadership (from the local to the national level) and the business community. As a corporate entity, the military is one of the largest consumers in American society. Military activities entail extensive purchasing, contracting, and interaction with business firms of all sizes. The military services have also produced a distinctive subculture with stringent demands on those who are to be labelled successful. All of these observations support the contention that we do in fact have a military *profession*.

The military can also be included under general descriptions of professionalism such as the following:

Professionals are expected to be persons of integrity whom you can trust, more concerned with helping than with emptying your pockets; they are experts who by the use of their skills contribute to the good of society, in a variety of contexts, for a multitude of purposes; they are admired and respected for the manifold ways they serve the growth of knowledge and advance [or protect] the quality of human existence. . . . [P]rofessionalism [is] an ideal defining a standard of good conduct, virtuous character, and a commitment to excellence going beyond the norms of morality ordinarily governing relations among persons.[21]

As we shall discuss shortly, members of the military frequently see themselves as answerable to a higher standard than members of the general population.[22] They also recognize that they possess unique expertise, and that they are to employ it only for society's benefit.

But we need to consider an even wider perspective. Most authorities would accept the following five elements as ones constituting the distinguishing attributes of a profession.

1. Systematic theory
2. Authority
3. Community sanction
4. Ethical codes
5. A culture[23]

The American military services appear to possess all five attributes, but that observation requires support. First, a specialized body of knowledge organized as systematic theory clearly exists. The areas of military expertise are leadership, strategy, tactics, weaponry, and logistics. The military educational system teaches these subjects systematically. And, in their area of expertise, military figures are accepted as authorities; the military organization, maintained and supported by a representative government, is clearly sanctioned by society. The nation supplies the military not only with the extensive material support necessary to an essentially "non-producing" activity (the military does not provide material goods or services for use by general members of society), but also with the people necessary to fill its ranks and accomplish its functions.

The ethical code is the subject we will turn to in the next chapter. Despite its uncodified status, a set of guidelines for conduct unquestionably exists for members of the armed forces.

While "culture" is a less precise term, we are all familiar with the concept of the military environment, which does indeed consist of specific "values, norms, and symbols." Special guides to behavior in social situations certainly exist in the military. The guidelines are not as rigid now as they were in previous generations, but they are extensive enough to fill books such as *The Officer's Guide* and *Service Etiquette*. Beyond the social rituals are the deeper norms of service with honor. And indeed the military probably finds its identity in symbols to a greater extent than any other group that might be termed a profession, especially if we accept that by symbols we mean "insignias, emblems, and distinctive dress; . . . heroes and villains; and . . . stereotypes."[24]

We have long associated one additional characteristic with professional activity—the idea that professionals are committed to their work in a special way. "The term career is, as a rule, employed only in reference to a professional occupation. . . . A career is essentially a calling. . . . Professional work is never viewed as a means to an end; it is the end in itself."[25] This characteristic is an ideal attribute, of course. It goes without saying that many lawyers enter the legal profession as a means of attaining social position or further opportunity. Otherwise, so many lawyers would not forsake their practices for administrative or corporate positions, or for the pursuit of political activity. Just as obviously, some medical practitioners are more concerned with financial benefits and social pursuits than the practice of medicine per se. As many career military officers probably find their occupation an end in itself as do members of the traditional professions. Because of the relative lack of financial and social rewards, the military may qualify as a profession on this account more clearly than a number of other commonly recognized occupations.

Professor Allan Millett has given careful consideration to the status of the military as a profession. As a result of a historical analysis, he concludes that

> by the time the United States entered World War I, the professionalization of American naval and army officers had taken observable form in the organizational sense. Both services provided line officers with mid-career training in fleet and army operations at the Naval War College (1884), the Army School of the Line and Staff (started as the Infantry and Cavalry School in 1881), and the Army War College (1901).[26]

Millett notes that while there is no fixed set of attributes of a profession, the following seem to be included in most analyses:

1. The occupation is a full-time and stable job, serving continuing social needs.
2. The occupation is considered a lifelong calling by the practitioners, who identify themselves personally with their job subculture.
3. The occupation is organized to control performance standards and recruitment.
4. The occupation requires formal, theoretical education.
5. The occupation has a service orientation in which loyalty to standards of competence and loyalty to clients' needs are paramount.
6. The occupation is granted a great deal of collective autonomy by the society it serves, presumably because the practitioners have proven their high ethical standards and trustworthiness.[27]

In the preceding discussion, we established that the military meets the first five criteria. That the last criterion applies forcefully to the military is perhaps most obviously indicated by the responsibility and authority granted to the military organization to administer a large percentage of public funds and resources, and by the fact that the military services have been granted the authority to operate separate judicial systems.

Despite the points raised so far, a critic might say that military career officers do not fit the tradition in which doctors or lawyers "hang out a shingle" and make their services available. That tradition is one in which a practitioner, possessing special knowledge and unique skills, is sought out by individual clients who put themselves in his or her hands. In this respect, the military professionals of today do not fit the pattern, for a single corporate client actually directs their activities. In fact, however, other professionals now increasingly depart from the traditional paradigm. Lawyers work for corporations, a situation in which the client becomes the directing employer. For many medical specialists, working for a salary or for a hospital or medical organization is now the rule. Professionals frequently work with particular institutional groups and in corporate settings in which all capital goods are owned by the organization. The traditional two-party arrangement—the professional and the client—no longer prevails as it did in the past.[28]

Moral Considerations

The security of the state has become a continuous concern at this point in the twentieth century, so much so that at times members of the government have cited the protection of national interests as sufficient justification for systematic deception of the public and lying to members of the House and Senate.[29] The increasing concern has led to a perceived need for a continuous military presence, which has undoubtedly furthered the development of a professional officer corps. The hallmark of such a group is the establishment of objective personnel management criteria based on ability, education, and experience rather than birth, social position, or political considerations. Morris Janowitz notes as well that

> a professional group is more than a group with special skill, acquired through intensive training. A professional group develops a sense of group identity and a system of internal administration. Self-administration—often supported by state intervention—implies the growth of a body of ethics and standards of performance.[30]

Military professionals unquestionably have a strong sense of identity, reinforced by a certain alienation from the society they serve. The military services have developed extensive systems of self-administration, and they profess a set of ethical standards and rules that have developed over time. Some members of the profession see the military as guardians of deep values rooted in national character.

If we accept that career military officers constitute the members of a profession in American society, moral questions concerning conduct in warfare and in preparation for war become more pointed and possibly more manageable. We can then identify morally troubling activity and morally ambiguous decision making as situations that can be analyzed in terms of role differentiation. Alan Goldman has shown that professional roles can be surveyed in terms of the degree to which the professional ethic renders permissible, required, or forbidden actions that would be judged otherwise under the criteria applying to members of society in general. Such differentiation can then be examined in search of justification. As I have indicated previously, one of the more plausible means of justification appears to be an argument regarding the fundamental values of society. That justification begins with the contention that professions exist to serve society.

Examining professional ethics in terms of role differentiation seems to be a reasonable way to reveal the moral structure within which military professionals work. I will apply this analytical technique in the discussion that follows. For those who believe professional ethics are grounded in moral truth in some sense, examining the justification of role differentiation may seem to be beside the point. I contend, however, that we can better understand the limitations on conduct imposed by the professional ethic by understanding the concept of role differentiation as it applies to the military.

Let me review briefly the points I have already made. The reasoning is as follows. The professional serves a social need in the performance of his or her function. One can thus argue that the status of being a professional, granted through society and its institutions, is a function of social needs. These needs are reflected in the fundamental values of society (though that is not to say that values are reducible to needs). In any particular society, special norms required by professional functions should be justifiable in terms of the basic values of society. That is perhaps the most significant aspect of being a professional and a professional group—the consequent existence of a particular moral relationship between the professional and the society within which he or she functions.

Because professions are social institutions, one obvious source of justification for professional activity lies in the values of society. Such values primarily determine social institutions. As the values of society govern the modes of social activity, so too the values of a particular group within society establish modes of activity for the group. One major feature of professional groups is that they have distinctive values generated by the professional activity, which tend to produce an explicit ethic. In many cases, such as those of lawyers, doctors, judges, and the military, special norms do govern the activity. To be rationally justifiable, the moral norms must be internally consistent, and they must be consistent with the values of the society which the profession serves. I think it is reasonable to maintain that if such consistency is achieved, one may conclude that, within the context of the given society, sufficient moral grounds exist for the special norms involved.

Chapter Three

The Nature of Professional Ethics

Other Professions

How does the American professional military ethic compare with other professional ethics that play important roles in regulating spheres of activity in our society? Before we examine more closely the influences that have shaped the American PME and the set of standards that now guide the conduct of members of the military profession, we need to consider further the nature of professional ethics in general.

The concept of professional ethics presents no mystery. A professional ethic is a code which consists of a set of rules and standards governing the conduct of members of a professional group.[1] The code may be a formally written published code, or it may be informal, consisting of standards of conduct perpetuated by training and example. While descriptions of what constitutes a profession may vary somewhat, all conceptions include the characteristic of self-regulation: "Every profession has a built-in regulative code which compels behavior on the part of its members."[2] And most professions recognize an ethic that is part formal and part informal.

Formally published codes are common today, partly because any group that desires the status of a profession appears to feel that having a publicized code of ethics is necessary to achieve that recognition. One formal code mentioned earlier, about which we hear frequently, is the lawyers' *Code of Professional Responsibility*, which consists of a set of "Canons," "Ethical Considerations," and "Disciplinary Rules." Published by the American Bar Association, the code provides a model for state versions, most of which have the force of law. The disciplinary rules establish clear-cut minimum standards of conduct. Violation of the disciplinary rules is often punishable under law. The ethical considerations establish interpretations of principles of conduct. They are aspirational in character and represent objectives toward which every lawyer should strive, but they also apply to many specific situations. The canons are very general normative statements concerning the standards of professional conduct expected of lawyers. All members of the legal profession should unstintingly serve justice, but how that is to be done in certain cases requires moving from the statement of broad ideals to the specific, concrete, grainy facts of particular circumstances. The ethical considerations and the disciplinary rules help serve that purpose.

The pattern of the lawyers' code is repeated in many other professions, including the Code of Ethics published by the Engineers' Council for Professional Development and the standards established through the American Institute of Certified Public Accountants.[3] The Engineers' code consists of four "Fundamental Principles," seven "Fundamental Canons," and fifty-six "Guidelines for the Use of Fundamental Canons." Its familiar structure follows the pattern of codes that consist of a statement of ideals, interpretations in terms of operating principles, and a listing of specific rules whose transgression is punishable through sanctions imposed by the profession. Altruism and social responsibility are not the only concerns reflected in codes. Some of the rules do not appear to have any broadly moral purpose — such as the engineer guideline that prohibits engineers from entering competitions for designs so as to obtain commissions for specific projects unless compensation is provided for all designs submitted. Such rules seem to further the self-interest of members of the profession.

Perhaps the medical profession has the longest tradition of adherence to a professional ethic, and we are all familiar with the existence of the ancient Hippocratic Oath. In the United States, the American Medical Association publishes the authoritative *Principles of Medical Ethics of the A.M.A.* which establishes general standards for professional conduct.[4] Section 1, for example, states that "the principal objective of the medical profession is to render service to humanity with full respect for the dignity of man." Section 9, which states the principle of confidentiality, is more specific: "A physician may not reveal the confidences entrusted him in the course of medical attendance, or the deficiencies he may observe in the character of patients, unless he is required to do so by law or unless it becomes necessary in order to protect the welfare of the individual or the community."

In the medical profession, an extensive informal code exists as well concerning day-to-day interactions among doctors, ranging from the handling of consultations and referrals to the status of medical competence of colleagues. Doctors learn those standards through the process of professional socialization.

Codes of professional ethics such as those I have mentioned serve at least three distinct purposes: (1) they protect other members of society against abuse of the professional monopoly of expertise, (2) they "define the professional as a responsible and trustworthy expert in the service of his client,"[5] and (3) in some professions they delineate the moral authority for actions necessary to the professional function but generally impermissible in moral terms. The first and third purposes are accomplished primarily by defining the rights and obligations of the professional in relation to clients, colleagues, and the public. Broadly worded references to responsibilities to humanity are common in such statements of general principles.

Thus the professional ethical code may both prohibit and permit various morally significant actions. The medical code professes high ideals, making adherents appear worthy of respect and trust, and identifies certain uses of medical knowledge as unacceptable. In many cases, the value to society of the professional function is such that, within the constraints established by (1) and (2) above, society authorizes the professional to perform actions forbidden to a general member of society. Doctors are entrusted to prescribe dangerous and addictive drugs, for example, and lawyers are allowed to conceal the facts of a crime when the crime was committed by a client. In an oft-quoted statement, Lord Brougham indicated the special status of the legal advocate more than a century and a half ago:

> An advocate, in the discharge of his duty, knows but one person in all the world, and that person is his client. To save that client by all means and expedients, and at all hazards and costs to other persons, and, among them, to himself, is his first and only duty; and in performing this duty he must not regard the alarm, the torments, the destruction which he may bring upon others. Separating the duty of a patriot from that of an advocate, he must go on reckless of consequences, though it should be his unhappy fate to involve his country in confusion.[6]

Members of the military profession also have a special status. Officers routinely initiate actions that will cause death and destruction. They are also permitted to constrain the exercise of fundamental rights in certain situations. We will have to examine such issues carefully in chapter 7, when we will consider the extent to which role differentiation in terms of moral norms can be justified for members of a profession. At present, I wish only to observe that a professional ethic will generally perform the three critical functions noted above: it protects society from exploitation, it enhances the image of the professional, and it may articulate a warrant for certain actions morally impermissible for a nonprofessional. The American PME serves all three purposes.

Formative Influences on the PME

The institutions of society are not formed in isolation. The concerns, interests, and objectives of the people involved with the institution will mold its nature. Once established, of course, a continuing institution such as the law, the government, or the military influences in turn the society which gave it birth. But there is no question that the generating society shapes its institutions. Thus one of the major factors that has affected the American military institution is the set of values that fundamentally characterizes American society. The Prussian army of the nineteenth century possessed very distinctive characteristics, as did the military forces of France when Napoleonic power was at its height. Members of the Japanese military leadership played major roles in Japan's politics until the end of World War II. Their attitudes and perspectives were strikingly different from those of the military services of the United States, even though essentially the same functional requirements affected their development.

Quite different rules and standards of conduct govern the military forces of different nations, which is to say that the military ethic varies significantly from one society to the next. While hardly an original insight, this fact is important because the most critical variable in each case is the culture of the society concerned. As values differ among societies, so, to some degree, do the codes of professional military ethics involved. Accordingly, examination of the values of the society concerned is necessary in analyzing a particular PME, for those values constitute one of the three major influences that mold a professional military ethic. In the case of the American PME, the values of society play an even more important role than they do in many other nations.

Guidance concerning professional conduct begins, logically, with the requirements imposed by the nature of the activity itself. With that in mind, we might disagree with the following claim: "It is my contention that the military cannot bestow legitimacy upon itself. This must come from society. If this is so, then the profession and professional values must be generally congruent with the values held by society."[7] While the military certainly cannot bestow legitimacy upon itself, this position appears to be too strong if "congruence" means complete agreement. Congruence is unlikely, particularly in terms of *priorities* among values, because of the exigencies of the profession; that is, because of the functional requirements involved in the systematic application of force. These are essentially constant from one society to the next, and their influence probably produces professional values that are not in complete agreement with those held by society. Compatibility, or noncontradiction, appears to be sufficient for legitimacy in the sense involved in this discussion—that of being sanctioned by society.

A study in the late 1970s revealed that most American military professionals felt that discipline, patriotism, and sacrifice are found "to a greater or much greater extent" in the military than in society in general.[8] Such a belief is not surprising if the military function imposes certain requirements concerning conduct. Samuel Huntington makes this point in his frequently quoted study, *The Soldier and the State:*

> The military profession exists to serve the state. To render the highest possible service the entire profession and the military force which it leads must be constituted as an effective instrument of state policy. Since political direction only comes from the top, this means that the profession has to be organized into a hierarchy of obedience. For the profession to perform its function, each level within it must be able to command the instantaneous and loyal obedience of subordinate levels. Without

these relationships, military professionalism is impossible. Consequently, loyalty and obedience are the highest military virtues.[9]

Without discipline, obedience will not be achieved. We can conclude, I believe, that the requirements of the profession demand loyalty, obedience, and discipline without any regard for particular social values. In the 1980s decade, members of the military are even more likely than in the 1970s to perceive the military as a more disciplined, more sacrificing group as compared to the larger society. Without dwelling on the justification of such views, we can reasonably claim that the exigencies of the profession influence—perhaps most pervasively—the content of any PME.

The third major influence arises from international law. Within little more than the last century, the laws governing the conduct of war have been codified and accepted by the states of the international community. The laws apply to all national military forces and thus constitute limitations on the conduct of their members. The regulatory guidance for American military forces specifically incorporates the laws, and the moral guidance makes adherence to the laws of war a duty. The laws of war themselves are grounded in moral principles, and those principles are specifically integrated into the PME through the incorporation of the laws of war. Thus, if such moral principles were not already incorporated into the foundation of the PME, they would be through the relationship between the PME and the international laws of war.

Given such disparate influences, can the resulting ethic be one that makes logical sense? If the ethic is to be practically useful in providing moral guidance for action, its provisions must not contradict one another. Otherwise, application of the ethic will produce statements that a given action is both right and wrong, permissible and impermissible. Any such code will be inconsistent and hence counterproductive in regulating activity within the profession.

The consistency of the American PME is thus in part a function of the compatibility of the three factors I have identified as the most important in the formation of the PME: the values of society, the exigencies of the profession, and the laws of war. These three factors have largely shaped the professional ethical code that guides the conduct of members of the American military.

A Partially Differentiated Role

The PME produced for the American armed forces by the three major factors describes the differentiated status of the professional activity. The American military professional fills what might be termed a partially differentiated role—one in which professional considerations will be given additional weight, so that in evaluating them in conjunction with general moral criteria, the moral balance may be shifted. To take an obvious example, general members of society would not sacrifice their neighbors on orders from the mayor. On the orders of superiors, military leaders may send their men into combat situations that make death certain for some, perhaps many, and their role as military professionals is clearly a factor in decisions to obey such directives.

For the military professional, the central goal of the profession is the security of the state, and the actual or potential use of force constitutes the means of attainment. For doctors, the central goal is the health of patients; for lawyers, it is the guarantee of justice insofar as the exercise of the legal rights of clients allows.

In pursuit of the central goal of the profession, the military in combat straightforwardly kill the uniformed enemy and directly cause widespread destruction of both government and private property. As a society, we consider such actions, within certain constraints, not only justifiable but obligatory. Underlying this fact in our society is the contention that in many cases the rights to autonomy and individual dignity represent higher values than the right to life itself.

Legally and morally permissible actions of organized military forces at times unquestionably override the rights of individuals. Enemy soldiers and civilians need not even be considered in coming to this conclusion. The rights to liberty and self-direction of an unwillingly drafted military recruit are subordinated to the interests of society when the interest concerned is military security and must be sought through conscription and mandatory military service. The legal right to free speech embodied in the First Amendment to the Constitution, generally regarded as a formalization of a moral right, is suppressed in peace as well as war for members of the armed forces. In such constraint, however, the right of free speech is not set aside. The right is still considered, but the decision maker gives greater weight to considerations involving security, morale, and discipline.[10]

And during wartime, society justifies noncombatant deaths and wide-spread destruction of private property (our own as well as the enemy's), so long as we honor the constraints of the laws of war.

Acts of violence, the possession of enormously destructive weapons, the imposition of discipline, and other aspects of military activity are morally and often legally impermissible for general members of society unless they are forced into a military role (e.g., a *levée en masse* or partisan warfare). Since certain actions expected of members of the military are morally impermissible for general members of society, the role of the military must be either fully differentiated (in which case only the professional ethic is to be considered in making moral decisions in the context of professional activity) or partially differentiated. If the military role were fully differentiated on the basis of functional requirements alone, and such differentiation were somehow morally consistent with serving society's interests, analysis of the ethical dimensions of the profession and the application of the PME would be relatively clear-cut. For the American military, however, military necessity and the demands of warfare are not the sole basis of the PME, which will be obvious when we articulate the provisions of the ethic. Both the values of society and the moral principles underlying the laws of war have affected the content of the PME. Because it appears unreasonable at first glance to conclude that the PME includes the entire structure of the American value system and the moral principles underlying the laws of war, one suspects that the PME is in fact partially rather than fully differentiated. Thus, while role-specific considerations may be given additional weight in making moral decisions, other moral considerations apply as well. This point is easily misunderstood, but I would argue that the American value system (which *does*, I think, include the principles underlying the laws of war) involves considerably *more* than the specifiable values, standards, and rules that constitute the PME. Although a professional code should help resolve certain kinds of moral conflicts generated by the professional activity, the provisions of the professional code and individual understanding of the code will sometimes be inadequate. Other moral considerations may apply in such situations, which suggests partial differentiation.

Both the officer corps and American society in general (and the Supreme Court, as reflected in decisions concerning military authority) recognize that those in a military role do indeed act with special moral authority in applying force on behalf of society. If that is so, partial differentiation certainly appears to be the appropriate classification for the professional role. In any case, the PME reflects the assumption that the differentiated role is justified. Whether the partially differentiated role actually is defensible is a question we will have to consider further in chapter 7.

In summary, the military professional, in the preparation for and conduct of war, takes actions which would not be permissible outside that role. The function of the military could not be achieved otherwise by the armed forces. Because of their special responsibility to society, however, military decision makers weigh the significance of their actions by the general moral criteria which derive from the basic values of society.

When individual moral rights are subordinated, some claim that there is sufficient justification in terms of preserving the fundamental values of society. Thus, if the foundational values of self-determination (freedom) and individual choice are subverted or constrained by specific alternatives, and officers weigh their special obligations and functional requirements against the violations of individual moral rights, such role performance constitutes partial differentiation. This, I contend, is the case with respect to the American military, and within the context of American society, the military considers such differentiation justifiable.

Military Values

That a professional ethic serves at least the three functions discussed earlier appears to be a reasonable claim: (1) protecting society's interests, (2) enhancing professional status, and (3) identifying special norms. These three functions together should facilitate the achievement of the purpose of the profession, so long as the profession in fact serves society (and if an activity or institution did not, in terms of our discussion, it would not be a profession). The three functions also appear characteristic of the American PME. A revealing 1970 U.S. Army War College study supports this view: "'Ethical behavior' and 'military competence' (knowledge of assigned duties) are closely interrelated and inadequate performance in one area contributes to inadequate performance in the other. This demonstrates the importance of professional ethics to long range mission accomplishment."[11] The long range mission is to protect American society and preserve the state under the Constitution. The PME thus facilitates this purpose, and the War College study suggests that the PME is essential to the primary mission. The quotation also suggests that certain types of behavior enhance the military function. We can describe such behavior in terms of "military values."

Concerns with the functional aspects of military activity have contributed to the formation of the PME. Huntington maintains that, over time, performing a certain role will produce distinctive habits of thought which give those who fill the role "a unique perspective on the world."[12] He defines "professional military ethic" very broadly as the "attitudes, values, and views of the military man,"[13] whereas I am using the PME in reference to a recognized set of rules and standards. Huntington's definition suits his purpose of sociological analysis, and he goes on to establish a model of behavior in terms of the "military mind."[14] The military mind, which I will refer to more neutrally as the "military perspective," is shaped in critical ways by military values, themselves the products of functional exigencies.

And what are "military values"? Are they values that presumably affect all military organizations? No one questions the military's responsibility for military security, which is the primary function of the armed forces and the reason for their existence. According to the analysis of Bengt Abrahamsson, a respected sociologist, this responsibility produces the following in any military organization:

- A view in which the state is considered the basic unit of political organization.
- A stress on the continuing nature of the threats to the military security of the state and the continuing likelihood of war.
- An emphasis on the magnitude and immediacy of the threats to national security.
- Advocacy of strong, diverse, and ready military forces.[15]

Huntington's research produces the same conclusion concerning the first item on Abrahamsson's list: "The military man . . . tends to assume that the nation state is the ultimate form of political organization. The justification for the maintenance and employment of military force is in the political ends of the state."[16] The idea of the military as an agent of the state is central to the professional military establishments in both Europe and the United States. From such a belief, Huntington says, it follows that, for the military professional, "the military security of the state must come first. Moral aims and ideological ends should not be pursued at the expense of that security."[17] State security is thus one of the primary values of a modern military force.

As one would expect, Abrahamsson's study of various national military institutions reveals them to be inherently conservative. "Military conservatism in part reflects dominant elements in 'classical' conservatism. It tends to emphasize order, hierarchy, and the 'stabilizing' institutions of society (church, family, private property). It maintains a pessimistic view of human nature and is dubious of the prospects for avoiding war."[18] Abrahamsson concludes that the most prominent characteristics of the military profession are the following:

- Nationalism
- Alarmism (the belief that armed conflict cannot be avoided indefinitely)
- Pessimism about the nature of mankind

Attributing pessimism to the military perspective is logical as well as empirically accurate, for, as Huntington points out, the military is charged with security. Viewing mankind's behavior from a standpoint that focuses on threats to security produces an emphasis on the acquisitive, egoistic, nationalistic, and aggressive aspects of human behavior. Such behavior constitutes the threat to security and stability that generated the creation of the military institution, and that behavior necessitates, both in society and in the military, organization and discipline in protecting society's interests. It should come as no surprise, then, that obedience and discipline are also primary values in the PME.

The military perspective reveals national sovereignty as a fundamental concept as well. The state, which legitimizes the professional military function, tends to be seen as an ultimate moral and political ideal. We commonly refer to this conception, of course, as nationalism.

Such are the reasons, in brief compass, for saying that the following aspects of the military perspective are directly traceable to the exigencies of the profession.

- •Nationalism
- •Pessimism concerning human nature
- •Pessimism concerning the possibility of eliminating war
- •Conservatism (emphasis on order, hierarchy, and social stability)
- •Authoritarianism (stereotyped obedience given and expected)

Empirical data supporting this view are highly persuasive.[19]

Within this military perspective, the functional requirements of military activity make certain character traits essential for sustained and effective operations.[20] These are the traits identified previously: loyalty, obedience, and discipline. Physical courage, or bravery, is another such character trait, and as we will discuss shortly, honesty or truth-telling in relationships within a professional group is a further essential characteristic. And no military force can be consistently successful against serious opposition unless it is technically proficient.

The exigencies of the profession, however, are but one of the three major factors influencing the formation and evolution of actual PMEs. The fundamental values of the given society will also affect the PME by changing emphasis and by establishing limitations on the determining influence of the purely "military" values in professional decisions. We will return to this issue in chapter 7. Each PME may have a different relationship with the international laws of war as well, so an understanding of any particular PME requires that it be examined carefully on an individual basis in its social and cultural context.

Chapter Four

The American Professional Military Ethic

The Sources

Not all young soldiers or young officers give serious thought to the professional ethics they are taught. Most simply accept that "the rules" are such and either attempt to abide by them or choose to violate them for reasons of their own. After a certain period of time, those who make the military a career begin to identify themselves in terms of their role, which makes their objective analysis even more difficult and less frequent. At least that was true in my case. It seemed obvious to me that military decisions involving moral issues were appropriately governed by the ethical code that structured the role of the professional military officer. The general precepts of the code were embedded in my moral awareness as a result of immersion in a firmly structured environment at West Point. The only issue was that of ensuring that one knew and understood just what the rules were.

Two years of combat service in Southeast Asia, however, generated numerous morally ambiguous situations, and the answers provided by the code as I understood it were sometimes incompatible with intuitions of conscience. In some of those situations, the code provided a rationale for overriding such intuitive misgivings. At some point in my experience, though, the code itself was no longer enough. Justification of the code became necessary. The nature of the conflict in Vietnam brought many soldiers to that point, I believe, and reactions to the experience varied widely. Disillusionment, cynicism, and resentment were not unusual ways of responding to the agonizing conflicts that abruptly and consistently confronted both willing and unwilling soldiers.

36

The first step in preparing career professionals for such problems is to make the code and its typical applications clear. The American PME has not been formally and systematically codified. The formal aspects of the code are found primarily in the oaths of enlistment and commissioning, the wording of the commission actually awarded to officers, and the codified laws of war, though a variety of official publications contribute to the accepted guidelines for conduct. Informal elements of the ethic are taught through professional socialization. For commissioned and noncommissioned officers, that process takes place most obviously in the structured programs of the military's professional development system, but the day-to-day activities in military units and the examples set by superiors provide the most telling influences. The role of military leaders at all levels is a critical element in the overall process of professional socialization. For example, the official policy of the military services concerning sexual harassment may be quite clear and specific, but if unit commanders indicate that sexual harassment is an unimportant issue and that harassment will be condoned, that perspective will dominate in the understanding of the informal code governing conduct. As the U.S. Army War College study noted, however, a definite consensus exists within the American military concerning professional ideals that apply to the military services.[1]

The Oath of Office

Broad parameters are established in the oath of office itself.

> I do solemnly swear (or affirm) that I will support and defend the Constitution of the United States against all enemies, foreign and domestic; that I will bear true faith and allegiance to the same, and that I take this obligation fully, without any mental reservation or purpose of evasion; and that I will well and faithfully discharge the duties of the office on which I am about to enter. So help me God.

The oath requires two commitments. The Constitution is the object of allegiance, to be upheld whether its authority is challenged from within or from without. Secondly, the officer is committed to perform the duties required in the professional role. Though the commitment appears straightforward, many officers give insufficient consideration to the political and moral principles manifested in the Constitution. Because the nature of the duties required in the role is open-ended, the professional officer's explicit commitment to support and defend the Constitution becomes particularly important. (In chapter 6 I will contend that it is this commitment that circumscribes the nature of the duties required in the professional role.) Commitment to the Constitution entails an obligation to the values and principles represented by the Constitution. Accordingly, the substance of those principles and values is critical to an adequate understanding of the American professional military ethic.

The Meaning of the Commitment to the Constitution

While it may be generally accepted, as I will argue, that characteristic values endure for any particular society, it is just as clear that values do change, if exceedingly slowly. If we consider the Constitution as the manifestation of the fundamental values of American society, we might be tempted to conclude that the values and principles that it is held to represent change with disturbing regularity. Analyzing the varying interpretations of the Constitution in court opinions has long provided a vocation for legions of legal scholars. As the political, economic, and social environment of our rapidly developing American republic changed, applications of constitutional law inevitably changed as well. Only through adaptation to new and unforeseeable circumstances could the Constitution continue as a viable blueprint for government. Aside from this obvious fact, however, the Supreme Court has been accused of imposing contemporary and transitory conceptions of morality in interpreting the Constitution. Such accusations appeared in Franklin Roosevelt's day and reached a crescendo during the era of the Warren Court. The matter again became one of national interest in the bicentennial year of the Constitution (1987) with the extended confirmation hearings for Judge Robert Bork, a "strict constructionist."

Despite such changing views, certain fundamental principles and values are as clear today as they were when the Constitution was written.[2] Interpretations concerning various aspects have altered—such as the authority of and relationships among governmental agencies— but basic principles and values have not. Constitutional scholars such as Leonard Levy support this contention: "Questions of constitutional law involve matters of public policy which should not be decided merely because of the original meanings in the Constitution. They must be read as revelations of the general principles that are expansive and comprehensive in character. Those principles and purposes are what was intended to endure."[3] The professional officer is particularly concerned with these principles. When officers commit themselves to the support and defense of the Constitution and acknowledge its fundamental authority as the basis of government, these basic principles and values are the object of their pledge. A brief examination of the way in which constitutional law changes supports the contention that the basic principles and values which underlie the Constitution are essentially constant. As one commentator points out, "The Constitution was not fixed for all time in 1789" but rather "is a set of fundamental ideas by which orderly change can take place in a stable society."[4]

The watershed era of the Warren Court probably represents the most significant shift in interpretation of constitutional law. As such, it provides the most obvious test of the contention that the basic constitutional principles change in application but not in essence. The positive constitutionalism of the Warren Court imposed new laws, in which the government was seen as having an obligation to take affirmative action to secure individual rights and liberties. Before the New Deal changed American life, and before civil rights became a national preoccupation, a different view of the government's role predominated.

> Both the Fourteenth and Fifteenth Amendments contain sections granting Congress the power to implement the Amendments' guarantees "by appropriate legislation." It had been a principle of Constitutional law since 1883, however, that this Congressional power was negative and corrective, rather than affirmative and preventive. In other words, nineteenth century Supreme Court decisions had established the doctrine that Congress' power was limited to the enactment of legislation to correct state actions which had already occurred, and which the Court found in violation of the Amendments' guarantees.[5]

The Warren Court introduced a momentous change from this view that has altered the character of American life in important respects, but the principle of individual rights itself has not changed. The major innovation of the Warren Court concerned how the principle of individual rights was to be implemented. The 1954 *Brown* v. *Board of Education* decision ended the long-standing precedent of "separate but equal" decisions and began the "affirmative action" era, but the content of the basic constitutional moral principles was unchanged. Whether individuals in general had certain rights was not the issue; rather, the question was the extent to which government at all levels must secure such rights against circumstances and events not in the scope of direct government responsibility.[6]

Rights and liberties are at the center of any analysis of the Constitution. The various political principles that structure American government—such as the allocation of powers between state and federal government, the separation of powers at the federal level, the checks and balances system, and representative legislation—all ultimately concern the creation of a system that protects the rights and liberties of individuals.[7] The Constitution has consistently been described in such terms: "Logically, the document is less a willful assertion of power than an act of sovereign self-restraint in behalf of a hierarchy of values that would find us willing to adjust our notions of economic well-being and national security as needed to honor constitutional rights."[8]

The concept of constitutionalism itself certainly belongs among the basic, unchanging principles represented by the central political document of the United States. The familiar preamble to the Constitution states that:

> We, the People of the United States, in order to form a more perfect union, establish justice, insure domestic tranquility, provide for the common defense, promote the general welfare, and secure the blessings of liberty to ourselves and our posterity, do ordain and establish this Constitution for the United States of America.

The preamble makes it clear that the purpose of the Constitution is to secure liberty, justice, and the general welfare. Constitutionalism holds that a written, comprehensible constitution that limits the power of government and of individuals and agencies in government is necessary for the maintenance of a civilized society in which citizens can enjoy liberty, justice, and equality. The body of the Constitution both establishes and limits the power of the specified branches of a republican form of government, and in doing so, reveals a profound wariness of the power of government. Because agencies of the government have command over extensive resources, the potential for the abuse of power is always present, as we know all too well from repeated incidents during the 1970s and 1980s. The "checks and balances" of the Constitution are an overt attempt to preclude or minimize such abuses. The principle of constitutionalism claims that, in the interests of liberty, justice, and equality, the constitution must be the final authority in the affairs of the state, embodying the fundamental values of the society in which it functions and reflecting the ultimate source of authority in republican government—the people. As established in the Constitution, the people—and only the people—have the indefeasible right to change their government. An understanding of the principle of constitutionalism helps clarify the critical importance of an officer's oath to support and defend the values and principles represented in our founding document.

The principle of individual rights is another of the fundamental values manifested in the Constitution, and it concerns those rights of man which are not to be denied either by the government itself or by the desires of the majority. The principle is reflected most obviously in the amendments to the Constitution and in the function of the Supreme Court, which is why nominations to the Court are closely examined. The Bill of Rights, the first ten amendments to the Constitution, reflects the doctrine of natural rights, which was the "hard core of Revolutionary political theory."[9] The Constitution forbids the majority or even the entire House and Senate to pass laws that impair fundamental rights of individuals. The strength of this prohibition is clear in the First Amendment: "Congress shall make no law respecting an establishment of religion, or prohibiting the free exercise thereof; or abridging the freedom of speech, or of the press; or the right of the people peaceably to assemble, and to petition the Government for a redress of grievances." An examination of the wording of the first ten amendments supports the well-documented claim that the Bill of Rights was originally "intended to render certain rights immune from abridgement by legislative majorities."[10]

In addition to specifying the rights of individuals to certain basic freedoms, the Constitution created the institution of the Supreme

Court. It is not implausible to claim that the powers granted the Supreme Court are primarily for the purpose of protecting individual rights—even, to a certain extent, against the will of the majority. Through this institution, the mechanism of government and law has a "limited mandate to correct mistakes made by State and natural majorities."[11] In so doing, the Court serves to protect the rights of individuals. The institution of the Supreme Court will eventually effect the will of the majority, but it ensures that action will be taken only after deliberate, reflective, considered study. Both the amendments to the Constitution and the institution of the Supreme Court embody the principle of individual rights within the framework of the Constitution.

While the preceding discussion makes reference to natural rights and the equality of all persons before the law, the Constitution governs but one nation—the United States. It applies to the regulation and protection of American society and the conduct of American citizens. To understand the implications of the oath to support and defend the Constitution, we need not be concerned with the more abstract elements of rights theory.

Whether we examine natural or civil rights, individual rights and social order in general are secured through the rule of law under an independent judiciary. If people are to live together in some regulated fashion, government must have the authority to restrict liberty, to regulate property, and to influence the pursuit of happiness—though such interference is permissible only under and within the rule of law. We find the principle of the rule of law clearly reflected in the Constitution and its applications in practice; one need look no further than the Due Process Clause of the Fifth and Fourteenth Amendments for evidence. Additional consideration reveals the interesting fact that while the president as commander in chief controls overwhelming military power, and while Congress controls the power of the purse, the power of the Supreme Court consists entirely in the principle of the rule of law established by the provisions of the Constitution.[12] Thus, we can reasonably claim that individual rights secured by law constitute the central value reflected in the Constitution.

Though we can categorize the provisions of the Constitution in a variety of ways, the principle of constitutional authority is indisputable. Closely allied with it is the rule of law. The object of both, it appears, is to secure the principle of individual rights, which is itself a basic moral principle. Of preeminent concern are moral rights. David Richards claims that "the Founding Fathers believed that the rights guaranteed . . . in the Bill of Rights were natural moral rights which government had no right to transgress. Man, they supposed, was foremost a moral person, and secondarily a member of a political union."[13] While natural law doctrine and the related concept of natural rights may no longer be the basis of legal theory in many cases, the idea of inalienable or natural moral rights remains. Discussions abound in which such rights are assumed to be self-evident. As we will note in our examination of the laws of war, human rights have become an increasingly prominent issue during this century in considering the moral limitations of governmental actions (though it has been disturbingly paralleled by increasing violations of such rights). In its most general form, the doctrine of human rights holds that there are certain individual rights that obtain quite independently of any particular states, societies, or time periods.

And indeed, this universal sense remains fundamental in the Constitution. The moral rights with which the Constitution is concerned "constitute moral reasons for action of a special weight and urgency."[14] They are "moral claims to kinds of individual needs and concerns which must be satisfied prior to other kinds of moral claims and which justify the use of force, other things being equal, in support of the moral urgency these claims involve."[15] Through the Constitution, these moral rights become legal rights as well. In that form, they are protected from unjust actions by the majority. Accordingly, "Majority rule is not the basic moral principle of the Constitutional order. The basic moral principle is the principle of greatest equal liberty. Majority rule is justified only to the extent that it is compatible with this deeper moral principle, which constitutes a standard of criticism for majority rule."[16]

This conclusion, supported firmly by the content of the amendments to the Constitution, establishes the relationship between the concept of fundamental freedoms and moral rights. The latter take precedence within the constraint of greatest equal liberty for all. The principle of greatest equal liberty guides us in moving from the abstract concepts of the rule of law and of individual rights to actual practice.[17]

While interpretations and applications of Constitutional law are perpetually in flux, firm ground exists for maintaining that the broad principles of constitutionalism, representative democracy, individual rights, the rule of law, and greatest equal liberty are fixtures in our national understanding of the Constitution. Also evident in our national history and implicit in the provisions of the Constitution, which authorizes the raising of armed forces, is the firm belief that these ennobling values are worth fighting for and that the use of force in their defense is fully justified. That is the soldier's purpose. When military members pledge to the support and defense of the Constitution, they commit themselves, by logical extension, to the principles and values that form the basis of its provisions.

The Commission

The commission provided to military officers begins with the following: "Know ye, that reposing special trust and confidence in the patriotism, valor, fidelity, and abilities of [named officer]. . . ." The commission from the commander in chief continues, stating that "this officer is to observe and follow such orders and directions, from time to time, as may be given by me, or by the future President of the United States of America." The fundamental law of the United States is the Constitution, so that the commission confirms the supremacy of the Constitution in the commitment of military officers. Were the president or any other superior to issue an unlawful order, military officers would be obligated by their role requirements to disobey it. That obligation finds its moral basis in the commissioning oath.

During President Nixon's last, bitter days in office, some people were concerned that the military might support an attempt by the president to remain in power despite the demands of Congress and the courts. Anyone who understood the commitment of the officer corps to the Constitution, however, would not have taken the possibility seriously. An officer's loyalty is to the principles and values manifested in the Constitution, not to the person of the commander in chief.

The oath and the commission provide the foundation for the traditional idealistic code of the United States armed forces—the code I have been calling the professional military ethic. The Armed Forces Code of Conduct, promulgated after the Korean conflict, also provides guidance for members of the military, but it has limited application because it concerns actions appropriate for those taken prisoner.

One note of caution may be in order at this point. The PME and actual behavior are two separate areas of consideration. That observation may be obvious, but frequently I find that discussions of what ought to be done in a specific situation relate both to prevailing forms of conduct and to ideal standards of conduct. Sometimes discussants confuse the two arenas and make the issue more difficult. The relationship between standards and actual behavior is complex; its study provides a fruitful subject for sociology and psychology, but it is not our direct concern here. One reason the U.S. Army War College *Study on Military Professionalism* caused such concern was the revelation of the gap perceived by members of the military between the recognized standards of professional ethics and real behavior. At some point, institutional pressures that require behavior which is inconsistent with the traditional professional ethic will result in a change in the content of the ethic itself. That will occur, that is, if the PME affects behavior at all. Elaborately formal codes in some professions sometimes appear to be designed for public consumption rather than self-governance.

The officers surveyed in the War College study, however, indicated that the "present climate" was at odds with the existing ethic and the exigencies of the profession. Moreover, I would contend that in some respects it was also at odds with society's expectations of the military. To what degree we can attribute the problems of the early 1970s to the protracted conflict in Southeast Asia is a subject of debate, but most army officers accepted the study as an argument for institutional reform rather than modification of the ethic. And reform followed, slowly, into the 1980s. The U.S. Army War College study summarized the issues in this fashion:

It is impossible to forecast future institutional climates with any degree of reliability. Nevertheless, it is not unreasonable to state consequences of the present climate: it is conducive to self-deception because it fosters the production of inaccurate information; it impacts on the long-term ability of the Army to fight and win because it frustrates young, idealistic, energetic officers who leave the service and are replaced by those who will tolerate if not condone ethical imperfections; it is corrosive of the Army's image because it falls short of the traditional idealistic code of the soldier—a code which is the key to the soldier's acceptance by a modern free society; it lowers the credibility of our top military leaders because it often shields them from essential bad news; it stifles initiative, innovation, and humility because it demands perfection or the pose of perfection at every turn; it downgrades technical competence by rewarding instead trivial, measurable, quota-filling accomplishments; and it eventually squeezes much of the inner satisfaction and personal enjoyment out of being an officer.[18]

Duty—Honor—Country

The discussion that follows focuses on the "traditional idealistic code" against which institutional effects are measured. We will examine the standards of behavior which military professionals feel they ought to meet, not conduct that fails to meet such standards or institutional pressures of a particular period that contribute to the failure to meet them.

To understand the code as it exists today, we need to remember its historical roots. In Europe prior to the nineteenth century, military officers came from the nobility. The tradition of the armed forces in America—where all men are considered equal—has been quite different.[19] The emphasis has been on ability and competence, which have been closely identified with character.

> Washington, almost from the moment of his death, became a legend symbolizing (among other things) the "superiority" of American military leaders over foreign officers because of their greater strength of character. Conversely, this rationale declared that officers who proved unworthy were probably so because of some character deficiency.[20]

Gen. Sir John Hackett, in his study of the American military, revealed another aspect of the professional officer corps. His comments also indicate that the pessimistic view of the nature of man and the likelihood of war has been a feature of the development of the American military:

The years between 1860 and World War I saw the emergence of a distinctive American professional military ethic, with the American officer regarding himself as a member no longer of a fighting profession only, to which anybody might belong, but as a member of a learned profession whose students are students for life. With this view went the acceptance of the inevitability of conflict arising out of the unchanging nature of man.[21]

The distinctive American PME that Hackett discusses is customarily referred to in a brief, simplistic motto. "The traditional standards of the American army officer may be summarized in three words: Duty—Honor—Country. The officer corps of today espouses this statement of professional ideals."[22] Analysis of what this motto means to the American military profession reveals considerable emphasis on individual character and certain virtues.

Duty. Duty incorporates the concepts of obedience and self-discipline previously noted in discussing the exigencies of the profession. While self-discipline would apply to most professions, it is of fundamental significance to the military professional, for the demands of duty can be particularly heavy. It may require the sacrifice of one's own life and the lives of others—an aspect of daily existence in a combat environment. The professional commitment is one of "ultimate liability." The requirement for both physical courage and the courage to make difficult decisions is implicit. In light of such demands, members of a military organization recognize that obedience is essential for effective functioning. As one long-time student of military sociology has said, "Integrity and instant obedience are the *sine qua non* of the military institution."[23]

In the American tradition, the oath of commissioning indicates that an officer's duty is to the state and, in particular, to the Constitution. Duty assumes the subordination of personal desires to the requirement generated by the oath—that of defending the Constitution and through it the state, in a specific form. "As a member of a service, an individual accepts a series of narrowly defined duties to superiors and subordinates consistent with his responsibilities to uphold that oath."[24]

Honor. For American military officers, honor connotes integrity, not military glory or prestige.

Its underlying values are truth-telling, honesty, and integrity. Implicit in "honor" is a sense of trust within the officer corps. Subordinates must be able to trust their leaders implicitly. The trust must be mutual if the unity and cohesion which are so crucial to combat effectiveness are to be developed. Requirements of combat demand high standards of honor, integrity, loyalty, and justice. The same applies to the military institution as a whole in carrying out the heavy responsibilities entrusted to it by the host society.[25]

The experience of recent decades sorely tested this aspect of the American PME. The substitution of appearance for substance, emphasized in the War College study, became obvious to profession and public alike in the Vietnam era. The allegiance of military professionals was not doubted, nor the general devotion to duty. The integrity of the officer corps, however, appeared problematic. The armed services have largely recovered from that experience, but the seriousness with which such developments are viewed confirms the central position of personal honor in the American PME. The actions of the two most visible military figures in the Iran-Contra affair, Lt. Col. Oliver North and Adm. John Poindexter, troubled many because they appeared to betray the PME. The arena of national policy in which the two men operated is considerably removed from the normal range of activity of a military officer, but they were still presumably committed to the PME. In that context, personal honor remains nonnegotiable. The following analysis states the position clearly:

At the daily working level, an atmosphere of trust and confidence is essential for military organizations to operate effectively. . . . Mutual confidence and esteem are essential to a unit's esprit de corps . . . high standards of personal integrity must be nurtured so that mutual confidence can survive long periods of stress.

When orders imply substantial sacrifice and risk on the part of subordinates, they must have no lingering doubts of the commander's true motivations. To execute the orders effectively, they must accept his personal integrity without question.

Of course, the most obvious and perhaps the unique requirement for high standards of honor in the military profession has to do with the necessity of accurate reporting in combat. The danger of unnecessary loss of life in such situations is too obvious to warrant elaboration. . . . The advice of the military professional to military or civilian superiors must accurately reflect current situations; otherwise, the consequences can be severe.[26]

While Lieutenant Colonel North, in deliberately misleading members of Congress and others in government about U.S. activities in relation to Iran and the Contra movement, was acting in the capacity of a presidential advisor rather than that of a military officer, the last paragraph of the quotation seems nonetheless forcibly applicable. That national security interests were undoubtedly damaged by efforts to serve the country makes necessary a careful examination of the last concept in the motto "Duty—Honor—Country."

Country. The country is the object to which the performance of duty and the maintenance of honor are devoted. This third element of the motto re-emphasizes the idea that no particular government administration or individual commands the allegiance of the military. The country itself (the state) is the beneficiary of the services of the armed forces. Further, members of the profession subordinate personal welfare to the welfare of the nation. This principle follows from the fundamental purpose of the armed forces. Since successful accomplishment of assigned missions often means that lives must be expended, the exigencies of the profession obviously demand that the means employed in combat, to include human lives, are precisely that—means. Because the function of the organization is critical, its welfare must have priority over the welfare of the individual members. Here again, however, the American PME is modified from the straightforward requirements of military activity, in which mission goes before all (which is to say that the security of the state justifies all). If functional imperatives alone provided the basis for moral decisions, the accomplishment of assigned missions would have priority over all other considerations. That, however, is not the case in the American military, as the discussions of the laws of war and the values of American society will illustrate.

The commissioning oath makes clear that the values of American society as exemplified in the Constitution give substance to the American PME. While human rights as such are not referred to in the

document, it establishes the political system in which individual freedoms, representative democracy, and equality are to be optimized.
Many of what we think of as human rights are reflected in the amendments to the Constitution, and the specifics of the Bill of Rights can
be justified in terms of the fundamental human rights highlighted
in the Declaration of Independence. The allegiance to country is
thus constrained by conceptions of morality and "guided by an overwhelming commitment to constitutional process."[27]

Traditional Values. Within the context established by "Duty—
Honor—Country," four other specific principles emerge that are also
fundamental to the American PME. The principle of professional
competence influences all professional activity in the American military. To the extent that any military organization becomes professionalized, technical competence becomes a central concern. "The nature
of the military profession, and the responsibilities of the profession to
the society it serves, are such as to elevate professional competence to
the level of an ethical imperative."[28] To conscientiously strive to perform in accordance with the precepts of "Duty—Honor—Country,"
an officer must be competent to carry out assigned tasks. The more
capable an officer is, the more successful he will be in living up to
the other principles in the PME. Given the weight of responsibility
shouldered by the military, no degree of competence short of the maximum possible can be declared acceptable in terms of the professional ideals.

Another fundamental principle is civilian control of the military
by the elected representatives of the people. From this principle derives another, far from unique to the American military but nonetheless basic to it. "The professional soldier is 'above politics' in domestic affairs."[29] If the integrity of the military is to be beyond reproach,
professional officers must not directly involve themselves in domestic politics. On the surface, such a position appears somewhat naive.
The military establishment is the largest institutional complex in the
government of the United States, and the extension of the "military-
industrial complex" in economic terms is most difficult to assess
because it includes so much.[30] Functional influence, however, is one
matter; overt participation by an individual is another. The code forbids the latter. While the distinction in practice is one of degree, the

services maintain it with surprising effectiveness. Certainly, the military as an institution traditionally observes political neutrality.

A fourth principle that is basic to the American PME concerns the importance of the welfare of the individual soldier, which goes beyond utilitarian concerns. Such a concept is to be expected in a society that traditionally has placed great emphasis on individualism. This principle is firmly embedded in the ethic as well as explicitly stated in the law. Article 5947, Title 10, U.S. Code, declares that "commanding officers and others in authority shall take all necessary and proper action . . . to promote and safeguard the morale, physical well-being, and general welfare of the officers and enlisted men under their command and charge." Two aspects of combat in the Vietnam era also reflect this concern for the individual. It was not unusual in the jungles of the Cambodian border area or in the mountains of the central highlands to find American soldiers in the field eating ice cream flown in by helicopters. While such actions might reveal logistical mismanagement, they also show the extent to which the system attempted to "take care of" soldiers. The second aspect was tactical. The massive use of firepower led to the concern (at times perhaps undue) with friendly casualties. Arguments continue regarding the degree to which manifestations of the concern with the welfare of members of society in uniform hindered the pursuit of military objectives, but that concern is firmly embedded in the American PME. In Vietnam, the attitude was epitomized by the dictum, "Spend bullets, not bodies." That policy was a function of public and congressional relations at some level, but "politics" was not the primary motive. Soldiers are members of American society who have value in their own right as persons. Lives of men and women in uniform are not to be risked without compelling cause.

The phrase "Duty—Honor—Country" thus represents the content of the American PME. Each term has particular connotations in the American context. The broad principles of civilian control of the military and of political neutrality overarch these connotations, and the obligation to promote the physical and psychological welfare of the individual military member to the maximum extent possible within the context of mission accomplishment permeates all aspects of the motto. Lastly, in each of these principles, the concept of professional competence is required and assumed.

Provisions of the American Professional Military Ethic

A specific body of rules supported by sanctions exists that applies to the military alone—the Uniform Code of Military Justice (UCMJ). Some might suggest that these rules are part of the PME. The UCMJ, however, applies to all members of the military, not just the most obviously professional component. It is more comparable to the laws of the state in relation to other professionals, which apply to professionals and laymen alike.[31] Nonetheless, the UCMJ defines honorable conduct in a negative sense by establishing what members of the military will *not* do. The PME, on the other hand, emphasizes ideals and positive aspects of conduct. Without question, the morality that shapes the PME also underlies the UCMJ, but the two guides for conduct are quite different.

The U.S. field manual, *The Army*, FM 100-1, establishes the army's position concerning professional ethics by identifying eight values central to the profession, divided into two sets of four each. The first set is referred to as the "professional Army ethic": loyalty, duty, selfless service, and integrity. The four in the second set are referred to as "individual values" that "strengthen the Army ethic": courage, candor, competence, and commitment. Integrity is generally accepted as an individual value, and competence would be included in any objective consideration of a "professional Army ethic." But while the division into two sets of values is difficult to defend, the set of eight values captures much of the PME.

The values of the profession thus identified and described provide a strong foundation for the uncodified tenets of the professional military ethic that does in fact guide the conduct of members of the military. But citing the values alone does not fully articulate the principles we have been discussing that derive from the Constitution. By joining these broad principles with the values listed in the field manual, however, we can formulate the "traditional ethic" of the American military as follows:

Professional soldiers
1. Accept service to country as their watchword and defense of the Constitution of the United States of America as their calling.
2. Place their duty first. They subordinate their personal interests to the requirements of their professional functions.

3. Conduct themselves at all times as persons of honor whose integrity, loyalty, and courage are exemplary. Such qualities are essential on the battlefield if a military organization is to function effectively.
4. Develop and maintain the highest possible level of professional knowledge and skill. To do less is to fail to meet their obligations to the country, the profession, and fellow soldiers.
5. Take full responsibility for the manner in which their orders are carried out.
6. Promote and safeguard, within the context of mission accomplishment, the welfare of their subordinates as persons, not merely as soldiers.
7. Conform strictly to the principle that subordinates the military to civilian authority. They do not involve themselves or their subordinates in domestic politics beyond the exercise of basic civil rights.
8. Adhere to the laws of war and the regulations of their service in performing their professional functions.

Because the American PME is uncodified beyond the designation of the eight values in the field manual and similar incomplete discussions in publications of the other services,[32] the exact content of the ethic will be a subject of dispute within any group of military professionals. I suggest, however, that in any formulation, these principles will find a place, though some further guidance may well be appropriately added.

If the eighth provision were not included, the American PME would be much less extensive in terms of content than the codes of other professions such as law and medicine. We have a short, informal set of broad principles based upon the oath of office, the commission, and American military tradition. Whether the American military professional should have a more extensive and detailed self-generated set of standards and whether a formally published, officially sanctioned code should be promulgated in addition to the current designation of the central values of the military profession are subjects for debate within the professional ranks. The eighth provision, however, represents a modification of the PME in the twentieth century—the incorporation of the laws of war. The PME becomes much more extensive and detailed as a result, and coherence becomes a more problematic issue. Are the laws of war consistent in themselves? And are they consistent with the other principles of the American PME? In one sense, the laws of war represent no more than another body of rules such as the UCMJ. In another sense, however, the laws of war represent a set of rules for applying certain moral principles. By incorporating the laws of war, the American PME has in fact incorporated the underlying moral principles. Accordingly, we must examine those principles if we are to understand the PME.

In the chapters that follow, we will examine the compatibility and consistency of the constraints on the behavior of military professionals created by the factors that molded the PME: the exigencies of the profession, the fundamental values of American society, and the laws of war. Most commonly in recent discussion—beyond questions about the morality of military activity itself—critics challenge the moral coherence of the normative guidance for the military in terms of the laws of war.

Chapter Five

The Moral Character
of the Laws of War

The Laws of War and Fundamental Values

Are there moral principles that provide a foundation for the laws of war? I believe there are, and that the American PME necessarily incorporates them when it incorporates the provisions of the laws of war into the ethical guidance for military professionals.

Regarding armed conflict in general, the states that constitute international society consider all combatants bound by the law.[1] The American military, however, has a closer relationship with those laws, as we discussed in chapter 4. From a legal point of view, the existing laws of war that are found in treaties and conventions to which the United States is a party expressly bind members of the American armed forces. Under the U.S. Constitution, treaty provisions have a legal force equal to congressional legislation.[2] And where no relevant treaty provisions exist in cases involving inter-state interests, U.S. courts apply as appropriate the customary law of nations. Part V of Department of Defense Directive 5100.17, 5 November 1974—the current official document concerning the DoD Law of War Program— states that "the Armed forces of the United States will comply with the law of war in the conduct of military operations and related activities in armed conflict, however such conflicts are characterized" (p. 1–8). Each of the military services goes further and issues its own implementing regulations.

As we have noted, one of the principal tenets of the American PME is unswerving adherence to duty. Requiring adherence to the laws of war as part of the duties of Americans in uniform brings to bear the moral principles that underlie those laws, which members of the American armed forces have a duty to apply whenever appropriate. Since no set of rules or laws can provide specific guidance for every eventuality, the "spirit of the law" may be the deciding factor in those cases in which the letter of the law is not specific or not applicable. That is merely to say that the principles which support the laws must be applied in order to reach a justifiable decision when the laws themselves do not determine appropriate actions. Accordingly, the principles that underlie the laws of war are particularly important for the consistent solution of new and unexpected problems not specifically covered by existing provisions.

To understand the American PME, we must attempt to achieve a clear understanding of those moral principles. Besides being necessary for some decisions, purposeful revision of the laws of war should come from such insight. With respect to our examination of the American PME, logical consistency will require that the moral principles underlying the laws of war be compatible with the moral principles derived from the fundamental values of American society, which play a major role in shaping the PME. To recognize that the American PME incorporates the laws of war provides only a starting point in examining the effect of integrating the moral perspective of the laws of war into the moral structure of the PME.

In order to clarify the relationship between the American PME and the laws of war, we must determine both the moral character of the laws of war and the fundamental values of American society that directly affect the American PME. Specifically, we must examine two areas: first, the nature of the laws of war and the relationship that exists between that body of law, if it is such, and particular moral principles; and, second, the particular set of "American values" that are central and enduring—those that would, over time, exert a continuous, shaping influence on the development of the American PME. We will turn to the second issue in the next chapter and focus here only on the characteristics of the laws of war.

Some legal scholars declare that "international law" cannot be considered law at all in any strict sense; that is a preliminary issue of some importance. All law is ultimately based on moral authority. If international law were no more than a form of circumstantially limited agreement, its influence on the coherence of the PME would be much less significant. The only moral obligation involved in adhering to the laws of war would be that resulting from the officer's commitment to the Constitution and to the PME. If the laws of war are ultimately based upon moral principles, however, then the officer is also morally committed to adherence to those principles, and it becomes necessary, in considering the coherence of the PME, to determine what those principles are. Most of the discussion in this chapter centers on that issue.

The larger significance of these issues is the degree to which they help answer the question of whether the moral principles underlying the laws of war conflict with or complement the fundamental values of American society. If those sets of values are not at least compatible, American military professionals could find themselves faced with paralyzing moral dilemmas in performing professional duties. The issue of compatibility is thus our primary concern.

Historical Development of the Laws of War

In a long historical view, with the understanding that armed hostilities must reach some level of significance to the society as a whole in order to be categorized as war, we can partially accept Karl von Clausewitz's general characterization that "war . . . is an act of violence intended to compel our opponent to fulfill our will,"[3] though war is no longer looked upon as merely a continuation of politics by other means. In the modern era, when the flames of conflict have burned brighter and spread more widely than ever before, the condition of war has become a complex technical status because of numerous treaties and the development of international law. What constitutes a state of war is not firmly or exhaustively codified by a universally recognized set of criteria, but international law has established that war is a "legal condition in which the [claimed] rights of a state are or may be prosecuted by force."[4] The U.S. Army's *The Law of Land Warfare*, FM 27-10, simply asserts that "war may be defined as a legal condition of armed hostility between states."[5] Including the concept of legality in these definitions serves to emphasize that war is a state of affairs governed by specified constraints—the laws of war.

Limiting how wars can be fought is hardly a new development. One historian notes that in ancient China, combat was conducted according to chivalric canons, and that land warfare in India during the same period was regulated by a body of rules found in the Hindu *Book of Manu*.[6] In Western society, limitations on the initiation of war trace their origins to the "just-war" theory developed in Christian ethics, though the instances of restrictions on armed conflict through custom can be found in the history of ancient Greece and the early Jewish tribes. St. Ambrose (339–397 A.D.) and St. Augustine (354–430 A.D.) are the best known proponents of the view that participation in war is justified only under certain conditions.[7] St. Thomas Aquinas elaborated on this theory, specifying three conditions necessary for just war:

1. War must be waged under the command of sovereign authority.
2. A just cause is required. Those attacked must be at fault.
3. Those initiating just war must have rightful intentions, which is to say they must intend to promote the good.[8]

Just-war theory, with many variations, has remained a subject of significant debate for centuries, though the terms "just" and "unjust" are now frequently replaced by the terms "defensive" and "aggressive." The most severe critics of just-war theory are radical pacifists who reject all use of force in response to violence.[9] Other critics of the theory base their objections on moral arguments as well.[10]

In addition to the concept of just war, which concerned *when* war itself was justified (*jus ad bello*), customs developed in Western society concerning *how* war was to be conducted once it was initiated (*jus in bello*). The customs and usages of war that came into being, though often honored in the breach, were widely recognized and accepted. The guidelines largely developed through practice. One can persuasively argue that the rationale for the development and observance of the laws and customs of war was prudential—an attempt to minimize the costs of war. Trade, human and material resources, and other economic considerations were also certainly major factors in support of mutually accepted restraints. Many customs endured because of strong common interest among opponents to keep limits on the conduct of war. The point is illustrated by instances in which restraints were not observed. One such example, amply recorded during the medieval period, is the Crusades. European nations did not consider the customs of war applicable to the religious wars against the "infidels," in part because no common interests between the adversaries existed.

The Dutch jurist Hugo Grotius (1583–1645), often referred to as the "father of international law," established the structure of the laws and customs of war that dominated for two centuries. Along with such seminal figures as Francisco de Vitoria (1485–1546), Baltasar Ayala (1548–1584), and Francisco Suarez (1548–1617), Grotius provided the philosophical and legal basis upon which the laws of war came to be accepted *as* law (albeit customary law) applying to all nations. Not until the later nineteenth century, however, were the laws of war codified in writing.

The codified laws of war now observed, which emphasize human rights, are a distinctly modern development. This fact effectively counters an observation offered in criticism of the claim that the laws of war have a moral basis. If we consider the rationale for the restraints imposed by the customs of warfare in the distant past, beginning with the Greeks and including practices from Roman times through the Middle Ages, we will indeed find little evidence of mercy or concern for human welfare. We do find considerable expediency and self-interest, which is sometimes taken as sufficient evidence for establishing the nonmoral nature of the customs and laws of war. To conclude, however, that the current laws are accordingly based on nonmoral considerations would be to mistake the motivations of those who promulgated and adhered to the customs and laws, both in the ancient past and in this century, for the substance of the laws of war. Those motivations do not necessarily reflect the nature of the laws themselves. And such a conclusion clearly overlooks the concern with individual rights that is now a central feature of the established laws and their application. Our codified laws of war can be traced to underlying moral principles, though nonmoral considerations are not to be ignored.

Interestingly, one of the cornerstones of the codified laws of war was emplaced in the United States.

The starting-point for the codification of the rules of war on land is the "Instructions for the Government of Armies of the United States in the Field" drawn up by Dr. Francis Lieber and revised by a board of officers of the United States Army at the instance of President Lincoln and issued from the office of the Adjutant-General to the Army as General Order No. 100, of 1863.[11]

The Lieber Code largely corresponded to the laws and customs of war as they existed at the time. The code was innovative in that it was the first example of a detailed manual for combatants concerning the conduct of war that attempted to codify customary law and standards applying to all nations. In Telford Taylor's view, "It [the Lieber Code] remained for half a century the official Army pronouncement on the subject, furnished much of the material for the Hague Conventions of 1899 and 1907, and today still commands attention as the germinal document for codification of the laws of land warfare."[12]

Soon joining the rules presented in the Lieber Code were the results of the efforts of J. Henry Dunant, founder of the International Committee of the Red Cross (ICRC). Dunant, a Swiss banker, had been overwhelmed by the suffering he had observed after the Battle of Solferino in northern Italy in 1859. The battle had left over forty thousand casualties. The war between the Austrian Empire and the forces of France and Sardinia lasted only from April to July, but the extent of suffering so impressed Dunant that he launched a one-man crusade against war and organized an international conference in 1864 in an attempt to mitigate the distress of combatants should war occur. The beginnings of the modern international effort to establish formal laws of war grew from that conference, which produced the first Geneva Convention. The major components of the subsequent development of the codified laws of war are depicted in Figure 5.1.[13]

The Existing Laws of War

The laws of war are a part of the body of law referred to as international law. Despite the lack of an established enforcement agency, international law has considerable force. "Today, most legal opinion throughout the world recognizes that international law is true law. Indeed, it would be difficult to hold otherwise since the world as a whole calls it law, regards it as law, accepts it as law, and expects it to be obeyed as law, even though the means of enforcing it are defective."[14] In fact, it seems clear in view of the Nuremberg Trials and the course of warfare since World War II that sanctions do exist for the laws of war, which form a part of international law. The sanctions consist of unilateral or multilateral retaliatory force and punishment, and the force of world opinion. Punishment of war crimes is required

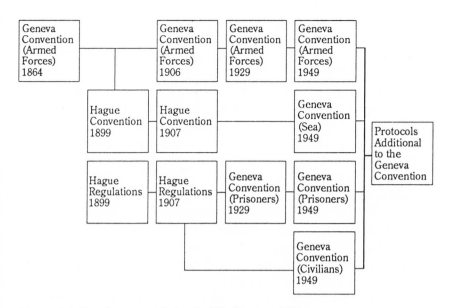

Figure 5.1. Development of the Codified Laws of War

of all signatories under the Geneva Conventions, and jurisdiction is properly exercised by any state having custody of the offender.[15] The sanctions may not be admirably effective, but they do in fact exist.[16]

An eminent jurist, Bert A. Röling, who served on the International Military Tribunal of the Far East, notes a common distinction made in terms of the Geneva and Hague conventions:

> Distinction is often made between the "law of Geneva" and "the law of the Hague," the law of Geneva giving rules for the protection and assistance to the victims of war, the law of the Hague giving rules for the prevention of people becoming victims. Stimulated by the appeal made by Henry Dunant, the Red Cross was established, and its primary interest concerned the victims of war. But the conventions adopted at the Second Peace Conference of the Hague, convened on the initiative of the Russian czar, in which many rules of warfare were codified, contained also rules for the protection of victims. A third impulse to the development of the laws of war originated in the human rights development. The General Assembly of the United Nations adopted several resolutions on "human rights in armed conflict."[17]

We can be even more specific with respect to the distinction: "The Law of the Hague comprises the St. Petersburg Declaration of 1868, the Hague Conventions of 1899 and 1907, the Geneva CBW Protocol of 1925, and the Hague Convention of 1954"[18] (for the protection of cultural property in the event of armed conflict). The law of the Hague largely concerns permissible means of fighting; the law of Geneva concerns treatment of the victims of war.

Before we consider the issue of the moral principles manifested in the laws of war, the sources of the laws of war need to be identified. The treaties and conventions to which various states have formally agreed constitute the most precise source of the laws of war. "This may be termed the statute law of nations; the law specifically enacted and reduced to signed documentary form. Particularly important are those treaties which have a great number of nations as parties . . . since their general acceptance demonstrates the generality of the principles which they contain."[19]

The most obvious source is the "customs and usages of war" that have developed and been recognized in the course of history as legally binding, comparable in nature to Anglo-Saxon common law. The legal profession and the courts have found both sources of law to be legal, binding, and practicable in application. Treaties create legal obligations for the specified parties but sometimes become so widely recognized and accepted that their provisions come to be considered "customary." That is the basis for the statement of the Nuremberg Tribunal in 1946 that "by 1939 the rules of land warfare laid down in the 1907 Hague Convention had been recognized by all civilized nations, and were regarded as being declaratory of the laws and customs of war."[20] The Nuremberg Tribunal observed elsewhere that

The law of war is to be found not only in treaties, but in the customs and practice of states which gradually obtained universal recognition, and from the general principles of justice applied by jurists and practiced by military courts. This law is not static, but by continual adaptation follows the needs of a changing world. Indeed, in many cases treaties do no more than express and define for more accurate reference the principles of law already existing.[21]

In addition to treaties and the customs and usages of war, we can identify two further sources of international law and its subset, the laws of war.[22] The judgments of both national and international courts (such as the Permanent Court of International Justice at The Hague) and *ad hoc* international tribunals (such as the Nuremberg Tribunal) have established principles and precedents that have contributed to the laws of war. Lastly, courts have recognized that those general principles common to all national legal systems also apply in the international arena. The charges in the Nuremberg Trials included wording reflecting this view: "The acts and conduct of the defendants . . . constitute violations of the general principles of criminal law as derived from the criminal law of all civilized nations."[23]

In addition to the Hague and Geneva conventions depicted in Figure 5.1, various multinational treaties and actions of the United Nations have contributed to the limitations in warfare. Two of the most important of these are the Geneva Gas Protocol of 1925 and the Genocide Convention established by the United Nations in 1948. The Gas Protocol was ratified by most major nations, though not until 1974 by the United States.

At present, because of the number of treaties and conventions codified over the last hundred years, the laws of war are largely in writing. Of those, the four Geneva Conventions of 1949, consisting of over five hundred articles, constitute a large part of the codified law. Those conventions almost exclusively concern the protection of war victims, such as prisoners of war and civilians in occupied territory. The Geneva Conventions have very little to say about the waging of war in terms of acceptable tactics and weaponry. The signatories intended the conventions to supplement the laws of war in view of the experiences of World War II. The 1949 conventions were ratified or acceded to by over one hundred forty states, though some have attached reservations to their accessions.[24]

The laws of war continue to evolve as the nature of war changes. In order to address issues that arose from the conduct of the war in Vietnam and other conflicts, the International Red Cross called for nations to send representatives to Geneva for conferences from 1974 to 1977. From those efforts emerged the Protocols to the Geneva Conventions of 12 August 1949. The two documents, Protocol I and Protocol II, were signed by sixty-two states in 1977, but the ratification process has been slow. The United States sees Protocol I as unacceptable because of its ambiguity and because its provisions would extend protection to terrorists at the expense of noncombatants. Neither of the Protocols have been ratified by the U.S. Senate.[25]

The ensuing references to specific portions of the laws of war provide a sense of their substance and content. In preceding paragraphs, as a beginning to our search for the moral principles that underlie the laws of war, I sketched the history and development of the laws. With an understanding of their factual character, we will be in a position to consider their moral character. The following excerpts are not intended to be comprehensive; they merely convey a sense of the substance of the existing codified laws of war.

The Beginning of War

The Contracting Powers recognize that hostilities between themselves must not commence without previous and explicit warning, in the form either of a reasoned declaration of war or of an ultimatum with conditional declaration of war.[26]

Article 2 of each of the 1949 Geneva Conventions adds to this provision of the Hague Convention and notes that the 1949 conventions apply to "all cases of declared war or of any other armed conflict . . . even if the state of war is not recognized by one of the parties," and also to instances of partial or total occupation. The laws of war thus come into play in all international armed conflict under the current laws of war, whether a formal state of war is declared or not.

When war is declared, each party to the conflict should name a "protecting power," which will help safeguard the interests of the warring party, primarily by serving as a medium of communication between the belligerents. The responsibilities of the protecting powers are set forth in detail in the Geneva Conventions of 1949. These imply a major role in addition to communication in that the protecting power is to be allowed to observe the conditions in which prisoners of war are held, particularly in response to complaints from the warring power whose interests it is safeguarding.

The Waging of War

Technological development has overtaken some of the provisions of the Hague Conventions, such as the prohibition against destroying submarine cables connecting an occupied territory with a neutral territory (Article 54, Hague Regulations, 1907). Reference today to satellite communications would be more appropriate. In a less direct sense, some of the general limitations established in the Hague Regulations (annexed to the Hague Conventions) have also been overtaken by changes in weapons systems. The requirement for "the besieged to indicate the presence of such cultural, medical, historical buildings or places by distinctive and visible signs, which shall be notified to the enemy beforehand" (Article 27, Hague Regulations, 1907)—the purpose of which is to enable the besieging force to meet the requirement that such buildings are not the objects of assault or bombardment— is difficult to observe in a combat situation in which ground-to-ground missiles with a seventy-five-mile range are routinely employed, or in which supersonic bombers flying at forty-five thousand feet drop bombs on targets throughout a belligerent's home territory. The status and protection of noncombatant shipping spelled out in treaties agreed upon before the introduction of submarine warfare have also been overtaken by the change in the means of waging war at sea.

The incompleteness of the laws of war as a result of new means of conducting warfare is particularly evident with respect to air warfare and aerial bombardment. Technological advances have been so rapid and so dramatic that the slow process of achieving consensus through usage has not begun to keep pace. The same is more obviously true of nuclear weapons, which are not even implicitly recognized in the existing laws of war, unless one decides to include resolutions of the United Nations General Assembly as contributing to the corpus of existing law.[27] The great imbalance of power created among potential belligerents as a result of exploding technological "progress" in weapons systems tends to make national self-interest the dominant consideration in international discussions of limitations on war. That imbalance has precluded agreement concerning the ways air and nuclear warfare are to be restrained and regulated by law.

We can, however, discern the intent of the limitations in the conventions established at the turn of the last century, despite the sections that are hopelessly outmoded. Further, the conventions have provided the substance of the laws of war, as indicated in the Nuremberg Tribunal conclusion mentioned before, on which convictions for war crimes have been based.

One of the most controversial yet influential provisions of the

Hague Conventions is the following: "The right of belligerents to adopt means of injuring the enemy is not unlimited" (Article 22, Hague Regulations, 1907). Article 23 continues by specifying that combatants are "especially forbidden"

a. to employ poison or poisoned weapons;
b. to kill or wound treacherously individuals belonging to the hostile nations or army;
c. to kill or wound an enemy who, having laid down his arms, or having no longer means of defense, has surrendered at discretion;
d. to declare that no quarter will be given;
e. to employ arms, projectiles, or material calculated to cause unnecessary suffering.

That these restrictions have been frequently violated is indisputable—but at least in some cases the violations have resulted in post-war criminal convictions. The conventions must be considered by prudent adversaries in conflict, even if, after such consideration, they are violated. The objections to the American conduct of the war in Vietnam resulted in part from perceived violations of Article 23 and other laws of war, and public opinion, both national and international, was largely responsible for the withdrawal of the United States from Vietnam. While what constitutes "unnecessary suffering" is not a matter of consensus, the topic is seriously discussed and is apparently of some importance in state policy deliberation and weapons development. Such points notwithstanding, considerable ambiguity exists. The U.S. Army's manual, *The Law of Land Warfare*, interprets Article 23e of the Hague Regulations in this manner:

> What weapons cause "unnecessary suffering" can only be determined in light of the practice of States in refraining from the use of a given weapon because it is believed to have that effect. The prohibition certainly does not extend to the use of explosives contained in artillery projectiles, mines, rockets, or hand grenades. Usage has, however, established the illegality of the use of lances with barbed heads, irregular-shaped bullets, and projectiles filled with glass, the use of any substance on bullets that would tend unnecessarily to inflame a wound inflicted by

them, and the scoring of the surface or the filing off of the ends of the hard cases of bullets.

The use of explosive "atomic weapons," whether by air, sea, or land forces, cannot as such be regarded as violative of international law in the absence of any customary rule of international law or international convention restricting their employment. (p. 18)

The existing laws of war appear to be regrettably incomplete in terms of providing guidance for the use of modern weapons. Interpretations or extrapolations such as those provided by the army manual attempt to bridge some of the most obvious gaps, though coherence becomes a problem, particularly with regard to nuclear weapons.[28]

During the 1970s, as I described previously, the ICRC launched a strong drive to prepare the "Protocols Additional to the Geneva Conventions of 1949." The 1949 conventions focus on the humanitarian treatment of service personnel and civilians in enemy hands and do not address the actual conduct of military operations. The ICRC project had the goal of updating the laws of war with respect to a broader application to all armed conflicts and modern developments in weaponry. Four international diplomatic conferences were held (one each year from 1974 to 1977) that produced the two protocols. Though the agreements have not yet achieved the full status of accepted laws,[29] it is interesting to note nonetheless that Protocol I addresses both the conduct of hostilities and the treatment of war victims, so that a merger of the "law of the Hague" and the "law of Geneva" seems to be in process. While adoption is still incomplete, the protocols represent the first comprehensive attempt since the Hague Conventions to limit the tactics and weapons permissible in war. The plight of war victims in World War II largely prompted the Geneva Conventions of 1949. The complexities of the Vietnam War, in which Americans pitted advanced weaponry against guerrillas and the forces of an underdeveloped nation, largely prompted the conferences that produced the protocols.

Certain constraints on the means of waging war can be traced to concepts presented by Immanuel Kant in the eighteenth century. The Lieber Code, in Article 16, placed limitations on the extent to which military necessity can be used to justify measures taken against the enemy in warfare, saying, "It [military necessity] admits of deception, but disclaims acts of perfidy; and, in general, military necessity does not include any act of hostility which makes the return to peace unnecessarily difficult."[30] The use of the term "unnecessarily difficult" leaves this claim open to varying interpretations. If an act is justified by military necessity (i.e., is necessary to subduing and defeating the enemy in some sense), how is such an act to be evaluated — moral considerations aside — in terms of making the return to peace "unnecessarily" difficult? Despite such ambiguities, Dr. Lieber was repeating the sense of one of the articles that Kant had presented in his essay, "Perpetual Peace." Article 6 of that essay, which proposed the provisions necessary to the achievement of international peace, declares that "no state at war with another shall permit such acts of hostility as would make mutual confidence impossible during a future time of peace. Such acts would include the employment of *assassins (percussores) or poisoners (venefici), breach of agreements, the instigation of treason (perduello)* within the enemy state, etc."[31]

This concept has resulted in a variety of specific rules, such as, "it is improper to feign surrender so as to secure an advantage" or to notify enemy forces that agreement to end hostilities has been reached when such is not the case.[32] Also, a flag of truce "must not be used to obtain time to effect a retreat or secure reinforcements."[33] Such rules fall under the principle that, outside of "measures for mystifying or misleading the enemy against which the enemy ought to protect himself, . . . absolute good faith with the enemy must be observed as a rule of conduct."[34] The U.S. Army manual, the source of the preceding quotations, explains the basis for this principle: "Treacherous or perfidious conduct in war is forbidden because it destroys that basis for a restoration of peace short of the complete annihilation of one belligerent by another."[35] The echo of Kant's article from the eighteenth century rings clearly.

The Treatment of Prisoners

Articles 4 through 20 of the Hague Regulations of 1907 concern prisoners of war, declaring that they "must be humanely treated." Details as disparate as mail processing and the exercise of religion are addressed. In the Geneva Conventions of 1929 and 1949 (see Figure 5.1), these provisions were considerably expanded. Article 13 of the 1949 conventions includes the requirement that "prisoners of war must at all times be protected, particularly against acts of violence or intimidation and against insults or public curiosity." Article 14 deserves being quoted in full to give the sense of the degree to which prisoners are to be accorded respect as persons under the current laws of war:

> Prisoners of war are entitled in all circumstances to respect for their persons and their honor.
>
> Women shall be treated with all the regard due to their sex and shall in all cases benefit by treatment as favourable as that granted to men.
>
> Prisoners of war shall retain the full civil capacity which they enjoyed at the time of their capture. The detaining Power may not restrict the exercise, either within or without its own territory, of the rights such capacity confers except in so far as the captivity requires.[36]

The 1949 Geneva Conventions, which complement the 1907 Hague Regulations but replace the 1929 Geneva Conventions (Article 134, 135, Geneva Convention—POW, 1949), cover almost all aspects of the operation of capturing, maintaining, and releasing prisoners of war, involving quarters, food, and medical attention, personal property, correspondence, labor and rates of pay, records, wills, repatriation procedures, and a variety of other details. This formal international consensus, containing 143 articles and 5 annexes, also carefully specifies who qualifies as a prisoner of war (Article 4).

Further, Article 3 of the 1949 conventions specifies treatment of prisoners and other noncombatants even in "armed conflict not of an international character." Absolutely prohibited are the following:

- Violence to life and person, in particular murder of all kinds, mutilation, cruel treatment and torture.
- Taking of hostages.
- Outrages upon personal dignity, in particular, humiliating and degrading treatment.
- The passing of sentences and the carrying out of executions with-

out previous judgment pronounced by a regularly constituted court, affording all the judicial guarantees which are recognized as indispensable by civilized peoples.

War Crimes

The Law of Land Warfare states that "every violation of the law of war is a war crime," applicable to any person or persons, military or civilian (p. 178). War crimes clearly include the "grave breaches" noted in Article 50 of the 1949 Geneva Conventions (e.g., "willful killing" of persons protected by the conventions, "torture or inhumane treatment," "extensive destruction and appropriation of property . . . carried out unlawfully and wantonly"). The U.S. Army manual also provides the following representative list of war crimes (p. 180):

- Making use of poisoned or otherwise forbidden arms or ammunition.
- Treacherous request for quarter.
- Maltreatment of dead bodies.
- Firing on localities which are undefended and without military significance.
- Abuse of or firing on the flag of truce.
- Misuse of the Red Cross emblem.
- Use of civilian clothing by troops to conceal their military character during battle.
- Improper use of privileged buildings for military purposes.
- Poisoning of wells or streams.
- Pillage or purposeless destruction.
- Compelling prisoners of war to perform prohibited labor.
- Killing without trial spies or other persons who have committed hostile acts.
- Compelling civilians to perform prohibited labor.
- Violation of surrender terms.

This brief discussion of the history, nature, and content of the laws of war provides the basis for consideration of our major concern—the moral character of the laws of war.

Underlying Moral Principles

We commonly acknowledge that moral principles underlie and constrain the activity of members of professions such as medicine and law. Whether the same can be said of the military profession is another question, and one likely to provoke debate. Because American military professionals are committed to a particular set of values as part of their professional status, the question in their case becomes one of identifying the values and principles. But any military group, I will argue, that is committed to adhering to the laws of war is also bound by the two underlying humanitarian principles:

1. Individual persons deserve respect as such (HP1).
2. Human suffering ought to be minimized (HP2).

These two principles differ in their schemes of justification: the first does not look to the consequences of deeds but concerns itself with human rights, while the second invokes utilitarian considerations and does depend upon evaluation of the results of contemplated actions. I contend that HP1 has priority over HP2 in the formulation of the laws of war.

Our brief examination of the content of the laws of war revealed the humanitarian concern that pervades the requirements and limitations established in their provisions. The "Martens Clause"[37] found in the preamble to both the 1899 and 1907 Hague Conventions indicates the spirit in which those two sets of constraints on warfare were promulgated:

> Until a more complete code of the laws of war can be issued, the High Contracting Parties think it expedient to declare that in cases not included in the Regulations adopted by them, populations and belligerents remain under the protection and the rule of the principles of the laws of nations, as they result from the usages established between civilized nations, from the laws of humanity, and the requirements of the public conscience.[38]

The United States Air Force manual concerning the conduct of armed conflict under the laws of war refers specifically to "the principle of humanity, which forbids the infliction of suffering, injury or destruction not actually necessary for the accomplishment of legitimate military purposes."[39] A subsequent passage states that "the principle of humanity also confirms the basic immunity of civilian populations and civilians from being objects of attack during armed conflict."[40]

Through the Martens clause, the Hague Conventions are founded upon the "laws of humanity and the requirements of public conscience." As the air force manual further points out, the Geneva Conventions in turn "safeguard such fundamental rights as freedom from torture or cruel and inhuman punishment; freedom from arbitrary exile; freedom from arbitrarily imposed punishment; and right to legal remedy for any abuse; right to minimum standards of respect for human rights at all times; and right to health, family sanctity and non-abuse."[41]

Those attending the Diplomatic Conference of 1949, which produced the four Geneva Conventions, affirmed that their work was "inspired solely by humanitarian aims."[42] The law of Geneva specifically concerns four primary areas under the heading of humane treatment for "protected persons":

1. Care of the wounded, sick, and shipwrecked
2. Treatment of prisoners of war
3. Immunity of noncombatants
4. Treatment of the population of occupied territory

All of the prohibitions and requirements in the conventions can be directly related to the protection of the rights of individual persons.

The Geneva Conventions thus specify measures required by the concept of human rights, which manifest the concept of respect for persons. Respect for persons entails the ideas of equality of consideration and human dignity. Individual persons cannot be treated with respect for what they are unless they are considered equally as persons (though that consideration obviously does not further entail equal treatment). To give preferential treatment denies the individual discriminated against the full status of a person—a rational being capable of independent choice and thus deserving of respect from other rational beings solely on the basis of that status. Human dignity is inherent in such a concept. In terms of modern ethical theory (and practice), the preferred means of establishing a framework for assessing the actions required in order to respect the status of individual persons is the delineation of fundamental human rights.

The principal thrust of the Geneva Conventions of 1949 is the attempt to specify the rights of noncombatants. The primary categories of noncombatants are (loosely) those disabled from fighting and those not directly participating in combat. Honoring their rights as required by the conventions is a moral and legal obligation for all signatories.

An examination of the Hague Conventions shows them logically consistent with the second humanitarian principle (HP2). They specifically concern the way to wage war. Article 23e, which prohibits the employment of weapons or material calculated to cause unnecessary suffering, and the Hague Regulations, which concern the protection of prisoners of war and civilians, were framed with the intent of ameliorating the evils of war.[43] The articles prohibiting treacherous or perfidious actions were devised to achieve the same end by avoiding the prolongation of war, which would probably occur if such actions were taken. Unless some minimal standards of conduct are mutually recognized, there will be no basis for settlement of the conflict other than complete victory and unconditional surrender. Almost every provision of the Hague Conventions can be seen as a direct means of minimizing human suffering, even though the motivation for establishing the conventions of war codified at The Hague may have been largely prudential.

Observance of the law of the Hague will in most cases cause less human suffering than would be caused by its nonobservance. That the law of the Hague manifests the first humanitarian principle (HP1), however, is not as clear. Whether a soldier shoots and kills an enemy with a standard .45 caliber round or with a .45 caliber round with a notched bullet appears to have little to do with respecting the enemy's status as a person. Such a constraint, however, clearly does have to do with minimizing human suffering.

While there are few provisions of the laws of war that are obviously attributable to only one of the two humanitarian principles, it also appears that HP1 and HP2 are nonetheless distinctly different principles that can conceivably come into conflict. A classic combat situation presenting problems of moral choice is one in which enemy soldiers are taken prisoner by a small force carrying out a critical mission behind enemy lines. By examining this type of situation carefully with respect to the two humanitarian principles, we can clarify the moral nature of the laws of war.

Consider the often-discussed prisoner case filled out as follows. The success of the small force in carrying out its mission will allow the seizure of a major transportation center without a significant battle which would affect a sizeable civilian population. If the battle does not occur, many combatant and noncombatant casualties will be avoided as well as extensive destruction of civilian property. The force carrying out the mission, however, captures several wounded enemy soldiers. The mission is such that accomplishment is not possible if the force keeps its prisoners in custody. If the commander releases the prisoners, the force will probably be compromised and unable to fulfill the mission. Under the circumstances, the commander of the force must decide whether to kill the prisoners and whether he can justify such execution.

We are particularly concerned not with his decision, but with the laws of war that apply to such a situation. In the discussion that follows, the two humanitarian principles will be applied directly to a situation involving choice among specific alternative actions. With respect to the laws of war as they exist, however, these two principles provide the basis for *formulating* the laws. Only in situations for which there is no applicable law or in which the justifiability of a particular law is in question would the principles be applied directly in determining appropriate courses of action. We should also recognize that there can be a conflict between HP1 and HP2 if we apply these humanitarian principles directly in deciding what to do in a given situation. In our hypothetical example, consideration of the question under HP2 indicates that the answer is "kill the prisoners," for in the short term this action will cause considerably less suffering than not killing them. Unless we assume some condition, such that the warring party to which the capturing force belongs would inevitably lose the war and that capturing the transportation center would only prolong the war with the result of increased suffering, the logical action under HP2 is to execute the prisoners and carry on with the mission.

One might object by saying that allowing the execution of prisoners will in the long run be counterproductive—that suffering will be increased by heightening the determination not to surrender and by encouraging battles and wars of annihilation. But if the prisoners are executed only in highly exceptional circumstances such as those presented in our hypothetical case, that objection is not persuasive.

Under HP1, however, the decision to execute the prisoners cannot be justified. If the leader of the capturing force is to respect his prisoners as individual persons, he cannot eliminate them solely as a means of expediting his mission, which he would be doing if he executed them. The prisoners, under HP1, have a basic right not to be treated cruelly or inhumanely. Both descriptions apply to summary execution.

The two humanitarian principles appear to call for opposite courses of action in the prisoner example—a situation that indicates that different rules would be produced if one or the other of the principles were considered alone in framing laws concerning the treatment of prisoners. Similar problems can arise if the two principles are applied directly. Some of the most obvious involve deliberate attacks on groups of civilians, use of weapons considered inhumane, and resettlement of civilians in occupied territories. We can hypothesize situations in which one course of action appears to be the logical choice if we desire to minimize suffering, while a different course is preferable if we are to respect individual persons as such. Our concern with the prisoner example and others like it, however, is that of first determining what the actual laws of war mandate and then identifying which of the two foundational moral principles underlies the existing law. The answers to two questions will thus clarify the issue. First, what do the laws of war permit or prohibit? Second, from what moral principle is the applicable law of war derived?

With respect to our prisoner example, we can find clear evidence in specific national regulations that are derived from the codified laws of war. Although the American manual, *The Law of Land Warfare*, written in 1956, does not specifically prohibit killing prisoners under any and all circumstances, the wording suggests that intention: "A commander may not put his prisoners to death because their presence retards his movements or diminishes his power of resistance. . . . It is likewise unlawful for a commander to kill his prisoners on grounds of self-preservation, even in the case of airborne or commando operations" (para. 85, p. 35).

The U.S. Air Force pamphlet *International Law—The Conduct of Armed Conflict and Air Operations* reflects the same position in referring to Articles 12–16 of the 1949 Geneva Convention Relative to the Treatment of Prisoners of War, but in more unequivocal terms: "These provisions prohibit killing or mistreatment of PWs whatever the military reasons . . ." (para. 13–2, p. 13–1). The laws of war, as construed by the United States, thus prohibit the killing of prisoners. This interpretation of the laws of war appears warranted and is shared by Geneva signatories. Accordingly, the laws of war that apply in the case of captured prisoners are derived from HP1 rather than HP2, for by applying HP2 directly, we found that the killing of prisoners of war could be justified in some circumstances. We must conclude, then, that HP1 has priority over HP2 in framing the laws of war in this instance.

In fact, such appears to be the case in all situations in which specific rights recognized in the laws of war are involved. In the three additional circumstances suggested previously (attacks on civilians, use of inhumane weapons, and resettlement), the applicable laws of war are based upon recognition of the rights of persons and thus derive from HP1. The most reasonable conclusion is that with respect to formulating laws of war in general, HP1 has priority over HP2, and "military necessity" is thereby limited as a justification for action.[44]

Our discussion shows that the laws of war govern practice under moral principles; accordingly, the legal rights established in the laws of war should reflect moral rights. Such rights derive from HP1, which generates the concept of rights in the context of the laws of war. Since the laws of war do prohibit the killing of prisoners, a prohibition consistent with HP1, one could again conclude that the two humanitarian principles have a priority relationship in which HP2 is subordinate to HP1. Further, as other examples of potential conflict between the principles indicate, it appears that HP1 will have priority in all cases involving recognized rights. The laws of war specifically recognize that prisoners of war have a right to be treated humanely and with respect as persons, which must certainly include the right not to be murdered. Therefore, the right of the prisoners not to be killed would have to be satisfied before the criterion of minimizing suffering is applied. Once we satisfy the nonconsequentialist principle, if more than one alternative law remains under consideration, we then turn to HP2 for further discrimination among possible laws.[45]

In sum, the two humanitarian principles that separately or jointly provide the moral basis for determining specific rules of conduct also define the moral character of the laws of war. The principle that individual persons should be respected as such can conflict with the principle that human suffering ought to be minimized. When that occurs, it appears there is a plausible argument for holding that the first principle (HP1) has priority. If HP1 provided the basis for justified participation in war, then HP1 is more fundamental than HP2. And if that is the case, only when the first principle is satisfied will the second be applied.

Because the laws of war are incomplete, and will probably remain so, establishing these principles and their relationship is important. Situations to which existing laws of war cannot be directly applied can then be analyzed in terms of the underlying principles, making resolution of problems more consistent and more appropriate. Lastly, though some commentators such as Richard B. Brandt consider a form of utilitarian theory to be the appropriate interpretation of the moral basis of the laws of war,[46] and would even argue that HP1 should be adopted for utilitarian reasons,[47] we have seen that HP2, which in itself can be considered a limited utilitarian principle, is more appropriately viewed as subordinate to HP1. HP1, in turn, is most plausibly seen as nonconsequentialist and thus not a utilitarian guideline.

The last step in our discussion of the laws of war becomes a simple one. If HP1 and HP2 reflect the moral character of the laws of war, then the two principles can be compared to the values of American society in our examination of the American PME. Our initial review of the values manifested in the Constitution, in which I claimed that rights and liberties are at the center of any such analysis, can be offered as evidence that incorporating the principles underlying the laws of war may not present a problem in coherence. Our discussion should also indicate the professional requirement for all members of the military to understand the limitations on action imposed by the existing laws of war. The more responsibility a member of the military has, the more stringent becomes the requirement to be fully informed about the provisions of those treaties and conventions concerning the conduct of war recognized by virtue of the Constitution's Article VI, Clause 2, which declares those agreements to be the "supreme law of the land."

Stating the role of the laws of war in the American PME is easier than determining what should be done in specific cases, as the prisoner example shows, so perhaps we should turn to another hypothetical situation to clarify the way that the laws of war shape permissible alternatives.

Case Study: The Pilot

Situation

Major Blue is a career air force officer. The unit to which he is assigned as a command pilot is based in a small country from which B-52 support is provided for American and allied forces fighting in another nation of the region. American ground units have been committed in that country to help repel an invasion from an adjacent state. The conflict, in which the United States is deeply involved though no state of war has been declared, has thus far been confined to the territory of the invaded state. The avowed purpose of American involvement is that of preventing the conquest of the invaded state and of restoring the territorial status quo that existed before the invasion.

Major Blue's wing has just been assigned the mission of bombing the capital city of the invading nation, and he has serious doubts about whether the mission is one that he can carry out. Specifically, the mission is as follows:

1. Destroy communications facilities located in a compound of government buildings in the center of the city.
2. Destroy an airfield on the west edge of the capital city which is the major reception point for war material supplied by nations supporting the invader's efforts.
3. Destroy a large warehouse section adjacent to the airfield but extending into the city where large amounts of war supplies are stocked, the most important of which are antitank and surface-to-air missiles.

The heavy air bombardment ordered is expected to cripple the enemy's ability to resupply combat forces. It is also expected to be a severe psychological blow, for this will be the first air attack on a populated area in the invading nation. American air power has previously been restricted to direct support of the allied ground forces.

The American strategy since joining the conflict has been to halt the invasion and to make the war too costly for the invading state to continue.

Major Blue believes American participation in the war is justified. The intervention of American forces, at the request of the invaded state and with the approval of the United Nations, was endorsed by Congress and is largely supported by the American public. Without the intervention, the invading nation would have overwhelmed the defending forces. In defeating the pro-Western state, the invading nation would also have gained control of waterways through which critical supplies of oil are shipped to the United States and other Western nations. American interests were clearly involved. From Major Blue's point of view, the intervention of American forces is both understandable and justified. The invasion has been halted, and the invading force has suffered serious losses that cannot be replaced.

The only feasible way to accomplish the mission with the B-52s is to run a bombing pattern through the airfield, the storage area, and the government compound. Air defense weapons around the capital are not considered a serious threat to the B-52s, but they would be deadly against aircraft at lower altitudes. The densely populated capital city will suffer heavily as a result of the raid. Extensive civilian casualties are inevitable. Fires and secondary explosions will undoubtedly cause widespread damage.

Major Blue has tried to suppress nagging doubts that arose when he was briefed on the warning order received by the unit, but he is troubled by the certainty that the civilian death toll will be extremely high. Such a result is not only apparently envisioned by higher headquarters but actively sought. In particular, Major Blue finds it difficult in this case to sort out the distinction between aiming at a legitimate target while running the risk of heavy collateral damage and aiming at nonmilitary targets in order to achieve the military purpose. Though he has such doubts, he is not at all sure what he should do.

Discussion

Major Blue may well ask himself whether the order is legal. He is bound by the PME and by regulations to adhere to the laws of war. Air force publications state that "the law of armed conflict applies to an international armed conflict regardless of whether a declared 'war' exists. This rule, necessitated by the law's humanitarian purpose and disuse of the legal status of war in international conflicts, is confirmed by international agreement and consensus."[48] If the order is in some way illegal, Major Blue is obligated to oppose or disobey it. The codified laws of war do not address clearly the subject of air warfare—except for archaic restrictions in the Hague Declaration that apply to the use of balloons—but the subject has received widespread consideration. Article 25 of the Hague Regulations (1907) states that "the attack or bombardment, *by whatever means*, of towns, villages, dwellings, or buildings which are undefended is prohibited." The emphasis on "by whatever means" was included to insure that aerial bombardment as well as other means would be limited by the article.[49] The American military, in seeking to clarify this provision, has declared that "there is no prohibition of general application against bombardment from the air of combatant troops, defended places, or other legitimate military objectives."[50] The capital city is guarded by a dense system of air defense weapons, and a number of army units are stationed there as well. Under the generally accepted sense of the term, the city can be considered "defended." Attacks on military targets in such cities thus appear justifiable in terms of the laws of war so long as "loss of life and damage to property" are not "out of proportion to the military advantage to be gained."[51] If the advantage sought is the inability of the invading state to continue the war, considerable loss of life can perhaps be justified.

One particular convention, Rules of Air Warfare (1923), applies directly to this situation, although it was never ratified. Nonetheless, the United States participated in the conference that produced the convention, and to a great extent, the rules are looked upon as corresponding to the customary rules of war in this area. Article 24(2) states that aerial bombardment

> is legitimate only when directed exclusively at the following objectives: military forces; military establishments or depots; factories constituting important and well-known centres engaged in the manufacture of arms, ammunition, or distinctively military supplies; lines of communication or transportation used for military purposes.[52]

One could argue that the communications facilities are an important part of the line of communication and that the airfield is part of the line of transportation for military equipment. Article 24(3) of the Rules of Air Warfare, however, seems to clear up such questions:

> The bombardment of cities, towns, villages, dwellings, or buildings not in the immediate neighbourhood of the operations of land forces is prohibited. In cases where the objectives specified in paragraph (2) are so situated, that they cannot be bombarded without the indiscriminate bombardment of the civilian population, the aircraft must abstain from bombardment.[53]

If this rule were accepted as part of the laws of war, the issue under discussion would be quickly settled. Unfortunately, in view of actions in World War II and subsequent conflicts, one may conclude that Article 24(3) of the Rules of Air Warfare has *not* become part of the "customary" rules of war, insofar as the prohibition against bombardment of civilian targets not in the immediate neighborhood of ground operations is concerned. Nonetheless, indiscriminate bombing of the civilian population is generally accepted as a prohibited act under the laws of war in any situation.

Further, the Hague Regulations require that "the officer in command of an attacking force must, before commencing a bombardment, except in cases of assault, do all in his power to warn the authorities."[54] This article is generally interpreted by the American military to refer only to places in which there is a civilian population,[55] but that is the case in our situation. Accordingly, the bombing mission as presented here appears impermissible under the laws of war unless warning is given to the invading nation that such an attack is to be made.[56]

If such a warning has not been given, it appears to be Major Blue's responsibility to bring this to the attention of his superiors. If the mission is not modified so as to render civilian casualties much less likely or if warning is not given, Major Blue is morally constrained by the PME to consider the mission order illegal and to refuse to obey. This conclusion is harshly demanding in terms of Major Blue's conduct, but it follows from both the circumstances and the PME. If the mission were legal under the laws of war even though civilian casualties were likely to be inordinately high in Major Blue's view, what action should he take—as a professional soldier? If appeals to his superiors were unsuccessful, what *ought* Major Blue to do under the PME?

First, we recognize that as a professional military officer, Major Blue has the responsibility to determine not only whether the order is legal but also whether it is morally acceptable. His first step in making that determination is to apply the PME. Major Blue must evaluate both objective and subjective factors in deciding whether it would be acceptable or unacceptable to carry out his mission under the PME. Subjective factors include the intent and motivation of the agent; objective factors concern the factual circumstances. If Major Blue carries out his mission with the motive of performing his duty in the most competent fashion of which he is capable, he can be confident that his action is justified from a subjective standpoint, for motive and intention are primary subjective elements. If he carries out his mission with the motive of avoiding conflict and the intention of furthering his career, his action may not be objectively wrong from a professional standpoint, but it is inadequate and unworthy in terms of the ideal standards of the PME.

Objective factors will be decisive in this situation as it stands. The action itself, aerial bombardment, is not immoral considered in isolation. Bombing as an instrument of war is acceptable, but how the bombing is done is a separate question. If in fact the technique to be employed is appropriately termed indiscriminate insofar as military and civilian casualties are concerned, the laws of war appear to prohibit the action.

Our discussion earlier in this chapter revealed that the laws of war limit the operation of the principle of military necessity. In the same way, the principle of proportionality identifies morally permissible actions—until specific provisions of the laws of war come into play. Then the range of permissible actions is limited by the existing law, even if the principle of proportionality would allow a wider range. Though ending the war in short order may well be considered an extremely valuable consequence of action, it would still be an inadequate justification for violating the laws of war. If a potent but short-lived biological agent were available that could decimate the entire enemy nation and bring the war to a rapid conclusion, it would still be morally and legally unacceptable to use it, for such use would conflict with the moral principles underlying the laws of war as well as violate the commitment of the United States not to employ such weapons. Indiscriminate bombing also violates those moral principles. It disregards the fundamental American values of equal consideration and respect for persons as individuals. In ignoring those values, the action of indiscriminate bombing violates the foundations of the PME. Accordingly, the action cannot be justified under the duty principle. It is morally unacceptable under the PME.

Indiscriminate bombing can also be described as knowingly aiming at nonmilitary targets for military purposes, which would be a violation of HP1 and again unacceptable under the PME because it incorporates that principle. What number of probable civilian casualties is unacceptable is also relevant to the objective evaluation. Bombs without guidance systems are clearly indiscriminate instruments of war. Once released from an aircraft, they can make no distinction between the military target and uninvolved civilians who may be in the target area through no fault of their own. The *use* of such weapons is the critical factor, for they may be used discriminately or indiscriminately. One civilian casualty does not render the use of a B-52 strike necessarily indiscriminate; fifty thousand casualties obviously would make it highly probable that the label was appropriate. Somewhere in between is a level at which the professional officer must draw a line. In any particular situation, a host of specific features will indicate where such a line is reasonably to be drawn, but the point is a matter of professional judgment. The authority to employ force in the defense of society carries the unavoidable responsibility for making such individual judgments.

Certainty in moral judgment is seldom attained in the complex situations which need the structure of moral evaluation sketched here. When a subordinate is certain that the moral judgment of a superior is wrong from a professional point of view, he or she is professionally obligated to take action. However, if the subordinate is uncertain of the correctness of his or her views in a situation in which professional judgments conflict—assuming no gross error is obvious and factual elements generating the respective judgments are recognized by the responsible commander—the judgment of the commander obviously takes precedence for the professional officer functioning under the PME. In such a situation, duty clearly requires obedience.

The difficulty of moral evaluation does not end here, of course. After analyzing the situation with respect to legal requirements and in terms of the PME, Major Blue still faces a third level of evaluation that involves his own beliefs. Persons of strong character are the ultimate resource for any military organization, and they are by definition persons of integrity—individuals whose actions are consistent with their beliefs. Major Blue must finally determine whether the actions he is ordered to take are consistent with his central moral beliefs. If he finds that the actions are clearly unacceptable, even if they could be rationalized under the PME, as a person of integrity he must have the moral courage to take a stand. Many years ago in Southeast Asia, I knew men in uniform who took a stand for moral reasons, and while I did not agree with them, I still respect them for doing so.

Discussion in this chapter has concerned the way in which incorporation of the laws of war generates limitations on the conduct of members of the American military in combat. The equation is not a simple one. We now turn to an even more complex subject: the relationship between fundamental American values and the PME.

Chapter Six

The Values of American Society

The Moral Framework for the American PME

Our discussion of the laws of war shows that they manifest humanitarian principles and, accordingly, certain values: human dignity, intrinsic human worth, and freedom from suffering. The American military, in adhering to the laws of war and in accepting them as legally and morally binding, implicitly accepts these principles and values as well. Together they form a part of the moral framework within which the American military functions, and thus they must be considered in examining the moral coherence of the American PME. The other major aspect of the moral framework consists of the fundamental values of American society, the subject to which we now turn. Within that set, distinctively moral values concern us in our examination of the role of American values in shaping and applying the American PME.

In chapter 4, I suggested that the Constitution serves as the documentary statement of our national values and that the interpretations of the Constitution, most formally through the rulings of the Supreme Court, serve to reconfirm its status as a bearer of national consensus concerning values. In the discussion which follows, I will turn to various sources that not only argue for that conclusion but also support my earlier contention that the fundamental national values reflected in the Constitution can be summarized as freedom, equality, individualism, and democracy. The meanings of those abstract terms require explanation as well.

Our discussion will provide the content necessary to apply the proposition that if professional ethics are to be justified by the values of the generating society, they must be consistent with those values.

If we can identify the fundamental values of American society, we can apply this proposition, and we can then come to a conclusion about the coherence of the three major influences that I claim have shaped and continue to shape the American PME: the exigencies of the activity, the laws of war, and the values of society.

American Values and the American PME

Any discussion of social or national values, unfortunately, will necessarily suffer from oversimplification. The attempt to attribute a specific set of values to a nation as large and diverse as the United States may well arouse skepticism. Any limited set will ignore internal oppositions and contrasts that are major factors in the life of a pluralistic society. For example, to accept equality in some sense as a fundamental value of American society without extensive discussion is to gloss over the fact that the United States began as a slave-holding society and is still characterized by strong racist attitudes and ethnic prejudices. Less than forty years ago, in 1954, seventeen states still had laws making racial segregation mandatory. We can find exceptions to any generalization involving a population that includes as many widely varying subgroups as we find in the United States. So long as the values we identify, however, can be reasonably verified and do not exclude important aspects of American culture that bear upon the nature and content of the American PME, our conclusions will have a reasonable claim to validity. And even though identifying enduring American values may prove difficult, I argue that anyone intending to justify or fundamentally criticize the professional military ethic must attempt to identify, understand, and apply that value set.

While it does seem intuitively plausible that "the concept of culture implies that there is a typical constellation of . . . orientations that form the basis for the behavior of most Americans,"[1] most of us would need more evidence to be convinced. Conflict between generations is often attributed to "changing values," which calls into question the assumption that accurate statements can be made about enduring national or social character. Among those who study the subject, however, many support the claim that characteristic, identifiable social values do exist for distinct national entities. David Hume's essay "Of National Character" suggests not only that distinctive characteristics can be expected but that they are inevitable:

> The human mind is of a very imitative nature; nor is it possible for any set of men to converse often together, without acquiring a similitude of manners, and communicating to each other their vices as well as virtues. The propensity to company and society is strong in all rational creatures; and the same disposition, which gives us this propensity, makes us enter deeply into each other's sentiments, and cause like passions and inclinations to run, as it were, by contagion, through the whole club or knot of companions.[2]

One might argue that eighteenth-century Europe can hardly be compared to the world of the twentieth century, but in the highly developed nations, information distribution and exchange is in fact incomparably wider than in Hume's day, rendering his thesis more plausible rather than less.

One can claim not only that there is a national character in the United States, but that it changes in glacial fashion:

> If an index of political culture is the content of public statements about America's values, norms, and beliefs, it seems reasonable to conclude that they have not changed significantly during the history of the nation. Presidents are still giving voice to essentially the same themes that were expounded by the writers of the Declaration of Independence and the Constitution. . . . Indeed, several very profound students of America's intellectual and cultural development have emphasized the absence of major change at this level. Louis Hertz, Daniel Boorstin, Henry Steele Commager, Ralph Barton Perry, and Robert McCloskey, all have claimed the American tradition to be essentially seamless and continuous.[3]

The same point echoes in the work of many sociologists, who note that in the midst of change there are nonetheless "common elements in all periods, and a definite and recognizable continuity in the course of development of the society. Some of the basic values and conceptions of the nature of man held at the birth of the Republic are still widespread and viable."[4] One respected researcher, Seymour Lipset, observes that "the value system is perhaps the most enduring part of what we think of as a society, or a social system."[5]

While standards of conduct vary noticeably over time and in different parts of society at the same time, the values upon which such norms are based seem to be much more constant. Those values produce and shape enduring social institutions. The fashions and temporary preoccupations of society certainly affect practice and behavior for a period, but the structures of social institutions are shaped by social values that persist over time. We can reasonably conclude that institutional ethics (such as the American PME) which derive from functional requirements and social values will be most deeply affected over time by values that are pervasive, predominant, and persisting.

Extensive research indicates both that certain values endure in society and that such values can be identified through empirical studies. I think of values simply in terms of criteria for choice, which is generally consistent with the more elaborate conceptions of sociologists.[6] Social scientists study typical modes of choosing. The considerations that preoccupy people in their daily activities are indicators of values. Conduct declared good or bad, in conjunction with operative social sanctions, also reveals the existence and nature of values in society. These and similar observations support the contention that the values of society can be empirically established and identified.

My concern in examining the influence of the values of society on the American PME is obviously to identify a system of valuation, or the enduring elements of such a system, that is applicable to military activity and whose ascription to American society is verifiable and largely noncontroversial. The subset of national values that we must identify is moral values—those that have an interpersonal focus or concern good and bad character. The moral values of society will exercise the major influence on the content of particular ethical codes within the society, and of those, what I have termed fundamental moral values will be most important. Unquestionably, within the body of American values as a whole there will be real and potential conflicts, particularly between moral and nonmoral values. In terms of consistency and justification, however, the fundamental moral values are directly relevant to our project.

The American Value System

For most of the nineteenth century, the majority of Americans were small landowners, and the family farm formed the basis of American life. This fact of social organization appears to have strengthened the individualism implicit in John Locke's philosophy, which in turn greatly influenced political thought during the Revolutionary period. Gerald Critoph sees this as a dominant aspect in the development of the American value system:

> Some of the major American democratic beliefs resulted from the experiences of the majority of Americans in agrarian settings during the formative years of the republic. For instance, the strong, abiding conviction that a free individual's identity should be held sacred and that his dignity and integrity should not be violated was a belief that came out of situations in which an individual had to confront the forces of nature just about on his own.[7]

Critoph's general observation refers to several of the values that seem to be included in almost all analyses of the American value system: democracy, freedom, individual integrity and dignity, equality of rights, struggle or competition, and achievement. The last two, of course, are not clearly moral values. The others deserve and require considerable elaboration if we are to address the issue of coherence confidently.

Freedom

Freedom is the watchword of democracy. The two concepts are so much a part of the American national fabric that it is difficult to stand back far enough to gain perspective on the issues. The thirteen colonies fought for freedom from British repression; the protection of freedom was the overriding consideration in creating the Constitution; and throughout our national history (the facts of particular cases aside for the moment), we have maintained that freedom and the preservation of democracy are the only causes justifying the use of our armed forces. Ralph Barton Perry maintains that although usually described as a "form of government," democracy is a social system and may properly be called an ideology—one in which the two fundamental values are freedom and equality.[8] The freedom that Perry identifies is "the principle of maximum freedom which is consistent with a similar freedom for all."[9] Freedom thus informs social institutions and in turn is "a product of organization—of the moral and legal institutions, which define areas of freedom, and guarantee them in the name of rights."[10] Just as democracy and freedom seem to be conceptually bonded in an inseparable way in the American tradition, so too are freedom and rights. In our democratic society, rights are the insurance of freedom.

The sociologist Robin Williams also sees freedom as one of our most widespread and persistent values, though he sees it as part of a pattern—a centuries-long process through which the restraints of feudal Europe were broken. In his view, events in colonial America were part of a larger sea change in Western attitudes, and in America,

the historical process left its mark in a culturally standardized way of thought and evaluation—a tendency to think of rights rather than duties, a suspicion of established (especially personal) authority, a distrust of central government, a deep aversion to acceptance of obviously coercive restraint through visible social organization.[11]

The peculiarly American sense of freedom presents no objection, Williams explains, to a situation in which the forces of competition and the marketplace result in a certain income or role for an individual, whereas any form of overt social coercion would be profoundly objectionable. "To be tied to a given locality by diffuse cultural pressure and lack of economic opportunity is regarded as a quite different kind of constraint from such controls as a police order or a governmental regulation."[12] Such an environment provides a foundation for a kind of economic meritocracy, with which we are all familiar. Those who obtain wealth, short of using disreputable means, are respected simply on the basis of being wealthy, and we consider them free to use their wealth as they see fit. This conception is in turn closely tied to a particular view of the value of equality.

Equality

Equality can come in many forms. The traditional American view is anchored in the Revolutionary period, when equality meant emancipation from a system of status.[13] The American sense of equality focuses on opportunity in that each person can make his or her own place in society and achieve whatever his or her potential allows. Equality of opportunity as opposed, say, to equality of distribution means that equal income or wealth is not expected or even desired. One reaps the benefit of opportunity in proportion to capacity and effort.

While not at all the same as equality of distribution, equality of opportunity—long the slogan of the "melting pot of the world"—does require society's support in the form of equality of education, social security, apportionment of the tax burden, and equality before the law, among other measures. Obviously, we can debate the degree to which even the ideal of equality of opportunity has been achieved in the United States, but we sincerely support that value as an ideal. And while "inequality of natural endowment is undeniable and ineradicable, and whenever the conditions of life are equalized, men will profit unequally by these conditions," in our society such conditions are considered "not only unavoidable but desirable."[14] Robin Williams explains the concept as a particular form of fair competition:

> The tautology that inequality is not resented unless considered to be undeserved takes on an important meaning, however, as soon as we are able to specify what "undeserved" means. By and large in the United States, it has meant *categorical* privileges (rewards not earned by effort and achievement) within the basic institutional rules for fair competition. Here is the core of the "American tradition" of equality. The dominant cultural value is not an undifferentiated and undiscriminating equalitarianism, but rather a two-sided emphasis upon basic social rights and upon equality of opportunity.[15]

This particular conception of equality is consistent with the value of individualism, with which the value of equality has a relationship of mutual dependence.

Individualism

The worth and primary importance of the individual (as opposed to the group, the community, the nation) in American culture undoubtedly results from a complex set of factors. Among them has to be the religious tradition in which every person has an immortal soul, even though religious beliefs no longer play the role they did in early American history. Freedom in America is freedom for the individual to live as he or she sees fit. Much of our law and many government institutions focus on the individual. Whereas some societies, particularly authoritarian ones, have emphasized the welfare of the collectivity over the welfare of the individual, American institutions are designed to protect personal freedom and autonomy. Our discussion of the Bill of Rights in chapter 4 emphasized the institutional bias toward the individual.

The intellectual individualism that has so profoundly affected American tradition can be traced to major figures in Western thought such as Thomas Hobbes and John Locke. In their differing views of social contract theory, in which men create and submit to governments as a means of furthering their individual interests, the autonomous, independent individual is the central figure. John Locke stated the claim clearly:

> Men being . . . by Nature, all free, equal, and independent, no one can be put out of this Estate, and subjected to the Political Power of another, without his own Consent. The only way whereby any one divests himself of his Natural Liberty, and puts on the bonds of Civil Society is by agreeing with other Men to joyn and unite into a Community, for their comfortable, safe, and peaceful living one amongst another.[16]

The focus on the individual in American culture produced the consistent emphasis on competition and personal achievement so evident in our history.

Democracy

The intrinsic worth of individual persons contributes notably to the values of both democracy and equality. As Williams suggests, the American concept of democracy rests upon an "implicit belief in natural law as opposed to personal rule, and the moral autonomy of the individual."[17] The idea that certain natural rights are inalienable is critical in a system in which we believe both that (1) the majority rules and (2) individuals are to be treated as "ends in themselves" and are thus considered equal to each other insofar as their status as persons is concerned. Democracy in America is a complex theme, one we can describe either as constituted by or as subsuming other values such as freedom, individualism, and equality. Democracy also implies a positive characterization of the nature of man (the people as a whole *can* govern themselves satisfactorily) and a belief in the possibility of progress.

The concept of democracy in this country is also invested with moral value, an aspect of our national values captured by Perry:

> The adherent of democracy rejects skeptical relativism and claims of truth. He refuses to concede that democracy is just one among conflicting ideologies, each of which is good for its own devotees. He claims it is the optimum form of social organization, endorsed by advancing enlightenment and acceptable even to present opponents in proportion as their ignorance, inexperience, or willful perversity is overcome.[18]

Because democracy, filled out by the values of freedom, equality, and individualism, has become an ideology, we tend to judge all other countries by our democratic standards. Nationalism and emphasis on patriotism have been the result, shaken only in any significant way by the deep divisions created by the events in Southeast Asia in the 1960s and 1970s. In many instances elsewhere in the world, nationalism itself has become an ideology that centers the total loyalty of the people on the nation-state.[19] Because we believe democracy to be the most enlightened and humane form of government, democracy as a value tends to clothe itself in nationalism.

Acceptance of nationalism as a social value usually includes an ideological commitment in which the particular nation-state is recognized as the ideal form of political organization. The existence of the state then assumes moral value in itself. While that is true of the United States to some extent, our national-patriotic orientation seems to conceive of patriotism "as loyalty to national institutions and symbols because and in so far as they represent values that are the primary objects of allegiance."[20] That characteristic saves us from the dogmatic form of nationalism that can be a severe threat to peace. Nonetheless, American nationalism, based upon the fundamental moral values we have discussed, is linked to the idea that "the American way" is a shining light that should lead to a morally superior existence. This quality of the nationalistic attitude reflects our general cultural tendency to see the world in moral terms.[21]

Part of the moral orientation of American culture has found expression in a persistent tendency toward humanitarianism, which will relate to my comparison of American values and the laws of war. Williams cites strong evidence for such a tendency:

> [Americans persistently demonstrate] a quick, impulsive sympathy for people who are in distress "by no fault of their own"; in anger at the overbearing individual, group, or nation; in pride in America as a haven for the downtrodden and oppressed. The proverbial generosity of American people toward other societies facing mass disaster . . . has elements of exaggeration and myth; but it does index a real and persistent theme.[22]

Sociologists readily admit that the subject of "social values" is of such complexity that research to date has been insufficient to support definitive conclusions. The relationships among values are not static, which unquestionably admits of the possibility of conflict even if changes in fundamental values occur slowly. Nonetheless, there do appear to be characteristic patterns of valuation that are generated by the culture of a given society. Also encouraging is the fact that there seems to be considerable agreement concerning the values that could be termed fundamental. Freedom, equality, democracy, and individualism are included in most serious examinations of American society. Extensive sociological studies involving surveys and questionnaires by Milton Rokeach, Norman Feather, and others support the contention that these concepts form the basis for a national value system whose substance can be established empirically.[23]

Democratic egalitarianism was proclaimed as a national ideal in the basic documents of the American Revolution and has remained such to the present day, though its manifestation has changed as we have become a technically advanced, industrial society. The Declaration of Independence, our statement of national identity, proclaims the universal rights of man. It constitutes the basic documentary confirmation of our natural law tradition: "We hold these truths to be self-evident, that all men are created equal, that they are endowed by their Creator with certain unalienable rights, that among these are life, liberty, and the pursuit of happiness."

This brief sampling of studies and informed opinion provides a reasonable survey of the values generally recognized as "fundamental" in American society. From a nation of Atlantic coast farmers and fishermen, southern planters, and western cattlemen, we have become a giant corporation which is in turn becoming an information-processing society. Still, the principles of individual responsibility and effort, achievement and success, and freedom of choice in a democratic system of equality appear to constitute the major underpinning of the American value system. The United States is a polity founded upon and self-defined in terms of these values and derivative principles, which are held to be universally true for all human beings.

Comparing the Laws of War and American Values

We can now compare the moral principles underlying the laws of war with American values in order to determine whether these two sets are conflicting, complementary, or indifferent with respect to each other. Such a comparison is proper since these are two of the primary influences on the provisions of the American PME.

I referred previously to the air force manual to emphasize the humanitarian aspect of the laws of war. In that connection, the same quotation also reveals the extent to which the Department of Defense recognizes the 1949 Geneva Conventions as concerned with the concept of freedom. The conventions, according to the manual,

> safeguard such fundamental rights as freedom from torture or cruel and inhuman punishment; freedom from arbitrary exile; freedom from arbitrarily imposed punishment; and right to legal remedy for any abuse; right to minimum standards of respect for human rights at all times; and right to health, family sanctity and nonabuse.[24]

The Department of Defense obviously interprets freedom in terms of rights, the traditional tendency in America. In an abstract sense, literal freedom is the capacity to choose without external constraint. In the world we know, the concept exists only as an ideal. The exercise of certain limited, specified freedoms, however, is generally a recognized human value, and in the United States it is firmly held. The listing of certain basic freedoms in the Geneva Conventions reflected the commitment of the formulating body to freedom as a value; I have previously described this commitment as implicit in the application of the wider moral principle that individual persons are to be respected as such (HP1). HP1 and the specification of derivative rights are fully consistent with the sense of freedom herein termed a fundamental American value. Personal freedom of choice is the foundation of moral responsibility, which makes freedom a moral value in the spheres of both the laws of war and American values. On this point, the laws of war and American values do not conflict.

Part of the concept of individualism in the canon of American values is the idea that every person is self-determining. Individuals are thus directly responsible for their actions. This view is closely allied with the concept of moral responsibility and the idea of freedom (or the exercise of freedom) as a value. Respecting individual persons as such requires restricting the exercise of one's own freedom so as not to infringe upon the capability of others to exercise a degree of freedom equal to that reserved to oneself. This requirement defines morally unacceptable infringements of the exercise of free choice by individuals, which demean the status of other persons as morally responsible agents.

In the context of our discussion, such infringements in the sphere of the laws of war are unjustified applications of physical force, where justification is limited to those actions by a national entity necessary for the equal protection of the ability of citizens of the state to exercise "free choice" or basic rights. In the sphere of national values, such infringements are the unjustified (in the same sense) applications of physical or psychological force through government agencies or social institutions as well as through personal relationships. Thus, the values of freedom and individualism found in American society and reflected in the laws of war appear to be in accord.

The sense of equality which HP1 embodies is that of a natural equality and, derivatively, equality before the law: all persons are to be treated and judged under the same standards. Without such treatment, respect for individual persons as such would be denied. The discussion of the American value of equality focused on equality of opportunity, but we base that concept on the idea that all persons are created equal in being entitled to certain basic social rights which are summarized in the rights to "life, liberty, and the pursuit of happiness." On the basis of these observations, we can conclude that the specific rights presented in the 1949 Geneva Conventions are fully compatible with the American concept of equality.

Democracy is a theme of variable hue, but if it is an ideology, as Perry claims, whose fundamental values are freedom and equality, there will be no obvious conflicts between the concept of democracy as a value and the principles of the laws of war. To the extent that democracy is considered a morally superior system providing the justification for radical nationalism and interventionist policies, however, it could present a potential conflict with the laws of war and the concept of defensive war. (In the twentieth century, the collective nations of the world, in conventions and United Nations declarations, have maintained that only defensive wars are morally and legally justifiable.) In addition, to the extent that we include humanitarianism as an aspect of American values, we find those values and HP2 in accord. Both HP1 and HP2 thus appear to be fully compatible with the moral values of American culture.

Nationalism—closely allied in the United States with our fundamental beliefs because we value freedom, equality, individualism, and democracy so highly—also constitutes one of the great threats to social stability and civilized existence. Radical nationalism does present the possibility of conflict with the principles underlying the laws of war. Many actions otherwise regarded as morally unacceptable can be condoned if nationalism is granted priority over other values and moral considerations. In a radical or dogmatic form, nationalism can introduce inconsistency into the values of American society. We have generally avoided that problem in the past.

The incarceration of Japanese-Americans during World War II provides an unfortunate example of what can occur when dogmatic nationalism and national security concerns outweigh the rights of individuals. In 1942, American citizens of Japanese ancestry were placed in concentration camps in the United States because of a vaguely conceived possibility that they represented a threat to national security. The action was taken under the authority of emergency war powers and was upheld by the Supreme Court, but the rights of this group of law-abiding and apparently patriotic citizens clearly were not respected, and the legality of the action is highly questionable. The choice faced by government officials appeared at the time to be between endangering the welfare of American citizens in general and violating the fundamental rights of a relatively small (and politically inconsequential) minority.

The type of conflict that most frequently arises for the military is one in which the professional must choose either to respect the rights of certain individuals or to achieve a particular objective that seems to be required by the commitment to serve society's interests. The potential for conflict is enlarged, because in any particular situation the interests of society as articulated by the state may not be in accord with the professional's private conception of those interests. Any resolution of such conflicts must specify the nature of the professional's commitment and must establish a priority among values. Since freedom is a fundamental American value as well as a value underlying the laws of war, the spotlight shifts from the laws of war to the realm of conflict among American values. For our present purposes, we need only observe that any conflict between the principles of the laws of war and the principles that are generated by American values undoubtedly exist for the American PME before the laws of war are considered.

Though our discussion has been brief, perhaps it is adequate to establish the following: (1) a set of values can be characterized as fundamental to American society as that society has developed, and (2) substantial agreement exists that freedom, equality, individualism, and democracy are basic moral values characteristic of American society as a whole. Commitment to "support and defend the Constitution" is thus also a commitment to the fundamental moral principles we have identified. Professional soldiers need to recognize the logic of that obligation and to understand its implications. While it is not the case that commitment by the military professional to the Constitution and the fundamental values identified here eliminates confusion in difficult choice situations (though it certainly helps), the nature of the pledge provides the basis for a strong argument that the American PME and the laws of war are consistent. If that is so, and if the fundamental American values are consistent with one another, the American PME appears to be morally coherent. Except for the possible dissonance created by the ethnocentricity of nationalism, which can be reinforced when it relates to the values of achievement and ideological democracy, the humanitarianism that informs the laws of war also operates in the American value system. HP1 and HP2 are consistent with the fundamental American moral values and thus with the principles to which military professionals are committed through their fealty to the Constitution.

One major consideration remains concerning our investigation of the American PME: the issue of role differentiation. If the three primary influences on the PME are consistent and compatible, as I have claimed, one can still reasonably question whether the role, which requires extreme departures from the moral behavior expected in normal social activities, is fully or partially differentiated. In chapter 3, I suggested that the role of a military professional is partially differentiated. In the next chapter, I will present my reasoning for that conclusion and thus will clarify priorities among the various factors that affect military decision making.

Chapter Seven

Justifying Military Decisions

Taking Stock

Before we launch into the subject of justification, it may be worthwhile to review the major considerations we have developed thus far. We have, among other things, examined the professional status of the career military officer, articulated the general principles that govern the moral conduct of members of the American military, and come to some initial conclusions concerning the compatibility of the three major influences on the American PME. We found that under most proposed sets of defining characteristics for a profession, the career officer corps qualifies as such. Our examination also revealed that the role of the professional officer calls for a deep commitment to a particular function critically important to American society: maintaining the security of the United States under the authority of the Constitution. The oath of office makes those responsibilities clear. As we find in parallel fashion in medicine and law, a fundamental value is ascribed to the central function of the profession for members of the American military. The commitment of the military professional is on behalf of a client—American society. Within the state, the government is the state's executive agency and the military is one means the government employs to execute policy and pursue national objectives. The military is thus an institution within an institution, serving a larger cause than interests internal to the military itself. Killing and other kinds of intentional violence are regulated in some form in all civilized societies. Without such regulation, society itself could not exist in any stable condition. The benefits of social existence could not be realized if violence against others were not curbed through law and convention. The military and police forces are exempted under law and convention from the prohibition against violence except in self-defense. Both groups are considered justified in applying force—even to the extent of killing—when it is necessary to enforce the law, in the case of the police, or to defend the state, in the case of the military. If the duty of the military, which consists generally in taking action to maintain the security of the state, includes killing other persons, it is accepted as justifiable in our society. Particularly in American society, where the dominant social values are moral values, the actions of the military are considered to have a fundamental moral justification—assuming, of course, that the actions are properly part of the effort to preserve the state and are part of a defensive rather than an aggressive policy or program. It is this moral justification that makes the American PME of singular interest. The nature of that justification has to do with the ends served by the military and with the state it protects.

Accordingly, as we have discussed, the military is characterized by a moral purpose which is supported through a professional code governing conduct. The code facilitates the accomplishment of the professional function. Within the context of a given society, the moral purpose justifies the profession, and in most cases, the professional function allegedly justifies the code. For the American military, we have established that the professional ethic is a noncodified traditional one that is perpetuated through the process of professional socialization. The PME is primarily the result of the influence of three major factors: the exigencies of the profession, the values of the society served, and the laws of war. We have seen that the moral principles underlying the laws of war are compatible with the fundamental values of American society, which eliminates one potential source of incoherence.

The claim I presented at the beginning of our discussion is the following: the role of the American military professional is a morally coherent, partially differentiated role that is rationally justifiable within the context of American society. I have thus far limited my argument for coherence to the reasonable contention that the fundamental values of American society and the laws of war are compatible. The next step in examining the American PME is that of considering the partially differentiated status of the military role. Can we confidently hold that it is justifiable from a moral point of view?

I believe that it is, given the following qualification: certain boundaries limit those elements of the PME that find their primary source in the requirements of the profession. The boundary conditions restrict military necessity and provide the moral coherence that might otherwise be questionable. I noted earlier that in most cases, the professional function for any professional group justifies the code which governs the activity. That is not true, however, of the American military. In the context of American society, it is not the case that a justifiable PME is one determined by functional requirements alone.

The three principles that are most obviously traceable to functional requirements are those of duty, truth-telling, and professional competence. Admirable though such characteristics are, the claim of justifiability can be made only if certain boundary conditions are recognized. Without the conditions, the PME becomes a predominantly consequentialist ethic oriented to mission accomplishment. Such an ethic produces results that conflict with our common moral intuitions and are inconsistent with fundamental American values. Not all members of the American military profession fully understand or accept such boundaries, which is why the issue is an important one. The principles of truth-telling and professional competence do not raise urgent moral questions, but the duty principle does. That, for the American military, is more than a functional requirement. Before we examine the duty principle itself, we need to set the stage by contrasting full and partial differentiation.

Differentiation of the Military Role

One way to reveal the differentiated status of the military role might be to consider the writings of authoritative members of the profession. Examining the writings of one such spokesman, Gen. Maxwell D. Taylor, reveals an ambiguous perception of the military role. His position and the views of others suggest that the moral end served by the armed forces in American society must be a central consideration in arguing the justifiability of differentiation.

General Taylor, in considering how military professionals ought to make moral choices, suggests that the appropriate choice is that which would be made by the ideal professional officer—"one who can be relied upon to carry out all assigned tasks and missions and, in doing so, get the most from his available resources with minimum loss and waste. Such resources might include men, money, weapons, equipment, allies, time, space, geography, and weather."[1] General Taylor's approach to ethical choice prescribes no specific rules. Instead, it suggests that the decision made by an officer of requisite character in the role would be the right decision.

Some structuring principles appear, however, as General Taylor continues. For example, he refers to the military professional as "a lineal descendant of the warrior who, in company with the king, the priest, and the judge, has performed throughout history a primal function essential to the survival and well-being of civilization."[2] General Taylor does not raise the concept of differentiation in his discussion, but he suggests that the officer's commitment to the security of the state is an overriding ethical consideration. If one accepts that the professional military function is "essential to the survival and well-being of civilization," such a suggestion is not surprising.

The following quotations from General Taylor's essay indicate the degree to which he sees broad moral rules as subordinate to the dictates of professional requirements:

> [A]n officer has little choice but to assume the rightness of a governmental decision involving the country in war. Having made this assumption, he is honor-bound to carry out all legal orders and do his best to bring the war to a prompt and successful conclusion.[3]

> Our model, recognizing that obedience to orders is one of the highest military virtues, one without which armies are worse than useless, will be instinctively inclined to obey any legal order.
> As for his attitude toward the voice of conscience as a guide to military behavior, he has serious doubts as to its reliability.[4]

What is meant by "conscience" in this passage is unclear. General Taylor elsewhere provides a variety of possibilities, such as a "God-given moral sense," "the voice of conventional morality," and "self-interest in a pious guise." The last suggestion is probably ironic, for there is a distinct difference between evaluations of what one morally ought to do and what will be of greatest personal benefit. People often rationalize and fabricate moral reasons for what they wish to do, but few seriously contend the two actions are one and the same.

Despite the status of ethical theory sometimes granted to egoism, few claim that that which is moral is exclusively that which an individual believes to be in his or her best interest.

General Taylor's other suggestions might well be considered labels for "ordinary morality," or the moral norms that apply to members of society in general. If so, General Taylor appears to be advocating a rejection of ordinary morality in favor of higher or overriding principles that derive from the professional function—that is, he appears to be advocating a fully differentiated ethic. Moreover, he seems to suggest that the functional requirements of the profession are the only appropriate basis for moral evaluation from a professional point of view. Such conclusions concerning General Taylor's intent remain purely speculative and may not be accurate. He may be supporting only a partially differentiated role, in which professional considerations are given additional weight in relation to the prescriptions of general moral criteria rather than being the *sole* basis of evaluation. But from his essay, it is not clear which position he would support. That ambivalence exemplifies the difficult problem of decision criteria that military decision makers face in a world of swiftly moving and dimly perceived events, when choices must be made, if only by default, and lives, even national fortunes, hang in the balance.

To encounter such a lack of clarity or a statement implying full differentiation is not unusual in discussions of this subject. We find sufficient variation and ambiguity among members of the profession to discourage a reliance upon any particular "authoritative" statement and to indicate the need for further study. I suggested earlier that the military role in American society is partially differentiated, but an advocate of full differentiation could argue that even though the fundamental values of American society have indeed shaped the PME, the PME itself, once produced, is the sole source of moral guidance appropriate for military professionals. Some might hold an even more extreme view, claiming that "a true soldier" will be guided solely by functional requirements.

In any military organization that intensively trains its members to be deeply committed to mission accomplishment and concentrates on developing the mental and physical toughness of its fighting force, more than a few of its members will conclude that winning is everything. And isn't that what we as a society appear to ask of our soldiers? Isn't that what we expect of our Marines? Don't we expect them to win, however tough the fight, no matter what it takes? The answer, of course, is no, we do not expect that, but between our national preoccupation with winning and the nature of much of our military training, we should not be surprised to find that many civilians as well as members of the military have received and accepted the message that military necessity rules when national survival is at stake. From there it is but a short step to believing that we must do whatever is necessary to win when we go to war. When one is fighting to preserve freedom and all that is good in human life, can anything short of total, unrestrained effort be justified?

Full differentiation would certainly simplify the task of making decisions about actions that affect others. No variety of moral perspectives is then involved; no complex utilitarian evaluation need be made. One merely acts in accordance with functional dictates acceptable under the rules for conduct in the fully differentiated role (though doing so may be controversial and demanding in itself). Then, adherence to the special norms of the profession would be recognized as justifiable regardless of the moral content of specific circumstances (in terms of general moral criteria). Still, to claim that actions may be justified solely in terms of the professional ethic or functional requirements is to take an extreme position. To determine whether such a claim is an ultimate "ought," we have to look *through* the specific actions to the moral ends served.

To examine the moral ends served by a professional activity in American society, we can proceed quickly by considering rights. Alan Goldman points out that "rights express interests important enough to be protected against additions of lesser interests across persons."[5] If this view is characteristic of a society, it follows that rights, or at least some rights, are absolute in relation to utilities, though rights themselves may be ordered—and must be, to resolve conflicts among rights. Such seems to be the case in American society. We maintain that protection of individual rights, however abused in practice and obscured by social complexity, is fundamental to a free, democratic society. The dignity and integrity of the individual can be realized only if the corollary principle of equal consideration of interests is defended. While equal treatment is not demanded (nor desired, it seems), the interests of each individual should receive equal consideration, from which it follows that within recognized and accepted parameters, equality of opportunity should be preserved. If the interests of certain individuals or groups are preferred by society's public institutions for reasons that are not morally relevant, the integrity of the individual is necessarily violated. And in a society which holds the integrity and autonomy of the individual as a foundational value, such violation will normally be both unjust and immoral.

How does this apply to our immediate concern? The moral end of the military, which serves the direct purpose of maintaining the security of the state, lies in the protection of rights which derive from foundational moral values. Only through such an end can ultimate moral justification for the military be sought. In the United States, the protection of rights is the moral end invoked, and the rights in question are those which the state exists to provide. Thus we find ourselves once more at the Constitution and the values it manifests. At a minimum those values include freedom, equality, democracy, and individualism.

An apparent contradiction results. To protect and preserve the values from which fundamental rights derive, it sometimes seems necessary to override the fundamental rights of certain persons or a particular group. But if the professional ethic governing such actions is to be morally coherent in terms of such values, it must at least be consistent with them. Explaining coherence requires a more searching examination of the issue of full versus partial differentiation.

The Case for Full Differentiation

The primary function of the American military is the systematic application of force. Force is employed to maintain the security of the state in the interests of the moral ends discussed previously. In considering the question of justifying differentiation, we can profitably ask whether the military professional can achieve the moral ends of the profession, and thus fulfill the social responsibility of the professional officer, without the status of full differentiation. We will first consider whether special norms are indeed necessary, and then how those norms should be categorized. Answers to questions in these areas may indicate how the authority of military professionals should be limited.

Throughout our early history, military security was largely assured by our geographic location. The oceans were major considerations in any strategic analysis. Formulation of the nation's foreign policy could begin with the assumption of secure borders. Twentieth-century warfare and modern technology have fundamentally altered the strategic picture, and the functional imperatives of military security now require capable, standing armed forces. "Fortress America," guarded by the Atlantic and the Pacific, no longer exists.

In contributing to military security, the armed forces provide what is apparently an essential service, and the performance of that service makes necessary specified relations with the rest of society. Such direction is required because the profession wields extensive influence over the welfare of the members of society, and moral guidelines help prevent the use of that influence to the detriment of the interests of society. For the armed forces, direction is found to a large extent in the operation of the professional ethic.

The American PME is an amalgam of law, custom, and tradition, the content of which we considered in chapter 4. In examining the justification for the ethic, however, we can consider some structural elements without regard to content. Legal statutes and codes provide detailed guidance for judges, for example, but the question of whether judges should scrupulously adhere to the law can be examined separately from the content of the statutes and codes that govern judicial actions. Further comparison of the situation of the judiciary as a profession to that of the military may provide some clarification of the issues involved. For the military, the principle of maintaining national security can perhaps be considered analogous in function to the principle of the rule of law for the judiciary. Maintaining national security is the *raison d'être* for the armed forces, just as maintaining the rule of law is such for judges. National security interests would then dictate the structure within which military decisions are made, just as the law establishes the structure for adjudication.

The apparently ultimate priority of national security interests brings into play the principle of necessity. Controversy has erupted in the past because of the precedence given to state self-preservation and to the protection of critical national security interests. In chapter 6, I mentioned the inexcusable treatment of Japanese-Americans in World War II. Military decision makers have been caught in difficulties similar to those of the government officials who decided to put the Nisei in camps in 1941. On the level of issues rather than personalities, the relief of Gen. Douglas MacArthur during the Korean conflict exemplifies such a controversy. General MacArthur's convictions concerning the actions necessary to pursue vital national interests brought him into dispute with his civilian superiors. The principle of subordination of the military to civilian authority was seemingly opposed to his obligation to pursue what he saw as the most effective course of action in successfully terminating the conflict. As a result of his views, General MacArthur, despite being America's best known and probably most highly respected soldier, was relieved from command of forces in the field. The principle of civilian control was upheld and strongly reinforced.[6]

Necessity at the highest level of national affairs is seldom the direct concern of the military professional; that responsibility lies with the national leadership. Insofar as international law is concerned, the principle of necessity provides justification only in those cases in which international law is breached in response to acts unlawful in character.[7] Insofar as moral justification is concerned, actions that are taken in the name of necessity are taken on the authority of the state. In such cases, justification of the actions must be in terms of the fundamental values of the society concerned, or the moral reasoning will indeed be incoherent. If the society is to be consistent, ultimate justification is clearly not a function of national security interests alone; rather, it is a function of the value system of the society. Ultimate justification must be moral, not legal or merely expedient. If it is consistent, such reasoning will provide rational justification for moral choices. Considerations appropriate for the civilian leadership of the state apply to the military leadership as well.

With these points in mind, we can pursue the issue of full differentiation and return to the comparison with the situation of judges. We can ask whether military professionals require special norms in carrying out their function as judges apparently do. We have established that such special norms are in effect. The authorization for killing and destruction provide the central case. The authority to infringe both individual liberty and the right of free speech is found in virtually all military institutions. To withdraw such powers—including the authority to employ force when called for in national defense—would be to render the military ineffective at best. If these authorizations represent a group of special norms, as they apparently do, we can ask whether the set to which they belong establishes a fully or a partially differentiated role. Parallels with the judiciary are suggestive.

Justice and equal status before the law are moral ends served directly by the functioning of the judiciary. The decisions of a judge materially affect the law and establish a precedent (in the Anglo-Saxon legal tradition) that has a formalized effect on subsequent judicial proceedings. This fact renders any degree of arbitrary judgment detrimental to the system. Judges must always remember as well that all decisions are subject to human fallibility. To interpose personal moral opinions in situations where all the facts can never be known and where the effects of such interpositions can never be accurately calculated would be to undermine the predictability and stability essential to the very functioning of the institution of law. All legal systems provide sanctions, but they operate on the basis of voluntary compliance with the law. If the vast majority of citizens do not voluntarily follow the law, the legal system could dissolve in chaos. A major component of such compliance is the expectation of predictability and stability.

These factors support the position that the role of judges is and should be fully differentiated, which is to say that they should adjudicate solely in accordance with the law, without regard to their own or other moral evaluations. They should do so in the name of the higher moral ends served by the institution of law—a conclusion based upon the functional requirements of their professional role. They are constrained to apply the law regardless of their personal views, and actions under such constraint are deemed morally justifiable, even if in specific cases they lead to results for the individuals concerned that are much less than optimal from a moral point of view. While we may not agree with this view concerning the role of judges (and I have doubts), it is a strong argument.

To what extent can a similar argument be made for the military? If one assumes that the actions of the American military under consideration are taken in the context of a just war, then one might argue that the actions required by military necessity are appropriate to national military security. We have established that it is not the case that *any* action can be justified by the principle of military necessity, but it appears that any action permissible under the laws of war which is also militarily necessary is indeed justifiable. One could claim that for a military professional to refuse to carry out such an action on moral grounds would be to betray the moral ends which the military is seeking to achieve through preserving national security.

One could then propose that the reliability achieved through discipline and obedience to orders is an essential characteristic of effective military operations. If the requirements of legal missions were subject to the moral views of individual officers, it might not be possible to achieve any meaningful level of reliability or predictability, which are as significant for the military as for the judiciary. Without reliability and predictability under the rule of law, the institution of law itself would not survive. Similarly, without the stability obtained by discipline and obedience to orders, one could argue that the military institution could not function and that national security could become subject to the will of other states or a particular group within the state. If discipline and obedience to orders are necessary for an effective military force, and if that force is necessary to preserve the value system of society, then it would seem that duty should override personal moral judgments. To refuse to obey orders on the grounds that certain actions are morally unacceptable or undesirable would be to set a precedent that could undermine military effectiveness in general.

Given such considerations, it does seem that the special norms of the military profession take precedence over moral considerations that would apply to a general member of society. (While I will argue *against* this view shortly, I want to present it fully before discussing my objections to it.) Professional soldiers can take actions, such as deliberately expending the lives of persons under their command in combat operations, which would be morally impermissible outside the professional role. The authority and the obligation for the pursuit of duty derive directly from the responsibility for the military security of the state. Thus it appears that special norms are necessary to the performance of the functions of a military professional. If the duties of the soldier, assuming they do not involve illegal activity, are not only justifiable but morally obligatory, then it is wrong for the professional to substitute personal moral views or the conduct morally prescribed for a civilian for the dictates of the professional norms. The conclusion of this line of argument is that the military professional is constrained in applying his personal moral beliefs to professional functions (just as the judge is constrained in applying the rule of law).

Yet another restriction indicates that the military role is differentiated, perhaps even to the extent of full differentiation. In discussing the role of the judiciary, Alan Goldman argues that an individual in the role of "member of society" is under no moral constraint with respect to the law.[8] Indeed, he claims that citizens in general should maintain a critical attitude toward the law. "Not only is one not obligated to give the fact of law extra independent weight in moral calculations, but it is not morally permitted to do so."[9] This is the case because "it is healthy for society to have the moral sense of citizens act as a check to the legislative power to command conformity with laws that may not always have moral ends."[10]

The soldier's situation seems clearly different—as does that of the judge—with respect to the pertinent laws, which are here the laws of war. Because of their role, soldiers have a moral obligation to act in accordance with the laws of war. The American PME incorporates the laws of war, which we have noted as being legally binding under the Constitution and the regulations of the services. Members of society in general, as noncombatants, cannot legally participate in combat operations under the laws of war.[11] Because the laws of war constitute a part of the American PME (as noted in chapter 4), we might consider this as further evidence of full differentiation.

The argument for full differentiation for the military professional can thus be made on the basis of at least four factors: the moral ends for which the professional institution exists; the necessity for discipline and obedience if the functions of the military are to be carried out; the operation of military necessity which overrides all localized moral considerations; and the moral obligation to adhere to the laws of war without substitution of independent moral judgment.

The Case Against Full Differentiation

Analysis of each of the four factors which seem to support full differentiation, however, shows that they provide an inadequate basis for such a conclusion. Justice and equal status before the law are moral ends served directly by the functioning of the judiciary. The military appears to differ significantly in that the military directly serves national interests by executing government policy. Such policies and interests, narrowly conceived, may or may not be in accord with the moral ends cited above. If recent history teaches no other lesson, it makes clear that national interests and national purpose, measured in terms of government action, have ranged the moral spectrum by the standards of the society concerned as well as of others. Only if the actions of a national government *are* in accord with the enduring, broadly conceived moral ends of society can the military function (in a society in which civil authority determines overall military objectives) be said to have "ultimate" moral justification. Consequently, such justification cannot be found solely within the purpose of the military, as seems possible in the case of the judiciary. Comparison of the effects of the military function with the moral ends of society is necessary.

Once such an accord is established, however, it can be argued that without obedience and discipline, the military cannot operate effectively. The implication is that the principle of duty is absolute in some sense. Frequently, in arguing what actions are appropriate in particular cases, military officers appear to assume that full differentiation is necessary if warfare is to be waged successfully. Similarly, one could suggest that the behavior of the fully differentiated role must be based upon functional exigencies alone. The situation of the military professional is closer, however, to that of the lawyer than of the judge in this regard. We can examine the differentiation status of the advocate role to see how this is the case. The role of the lawyer also provides some useful insight into the question of the differentiation status of the military.

The American Bar Association *Code of Professional Responsibility* requires a lawyer to pursue a client's interests without exception within the limits of the law.[12] This is the "received view" which has dominated since Lord Brougham's day. The traditional interpretation of the principle of full advocacy implies a fully differentiated role similar to that of the judiciary. Goldman argues that such a view is unwarranted.

The operation of the principle of full advocacy in our adversary system of law reflects one of the fundamental values of American society that we discussed earlier, "protection of individual dignity and autonomy, even at the expense of collective public welfare, is pervasive in our legal system, as that institution reflects our deeper rights-based moral framework."[13] To accept full advocacy solely on this basis, however, would be premature. To do so would be to affirm complete role differentiation, because those actions required by service to a client that were impermissible under general moral criteria would nonetheless be justifiable and obligatory for lawyers. Several considerations suggest that the principle of full advocacy should be modified by the dictates of ordinary morality.[14]

Normally, the wrong of punishing the innocent outweighs the wrong of failing to provide maximum protection to the public in general. When the guilt of the accused is actual and confirmed, however, or when the harm to innocent persons that will result from full advocacy is greater than the considerations of principle in providing the accused with the most rigorous defense possible, some actions apparently justified by the code under the principle of full advocacy may be properly ruled out by general moral principles. In this view,

> lawyers are not, therefore, justified in using all those tactics to secure acquittal, including presentation of false testimony, harmfully aggressive cross examination, or impeachment of testimony of truthful witnesses, that they might be justified in using to prevent conviction of an innocent client.[15]

If that is so, the role of the lawyer is partially rather than fully differentiated.

Strong arguments can be made for both sides of this question in the realm of criminal law, but in the context of corporate law, the principle of full advocacy no longer applies in the same sense. As a functioning part of the corporate entity, the corporation lawyer is no longer a disinterested advocate. To a significant extent, he or she is representing personal interests. In addition, as corporations influence the law itself through the lobbying activities of their legal divisions, the adequacy of the restriction to actions within the law becomes questionable.[16] Much of the legal activity on behalf of corporations is not conducted in an adversarial context. The purpose of the principle of full advocacy, which assumes vigorous and informed pursuit of opposing interests, will often be morally inappropriate. For example, those whose interests are in jeopardy (the public) are not represented when lawyers lobby to weaken regulations controlling the safe manufacture of drugs. In such a case, which is outside the criminal justice system, it is even more obvious that moral considerations other than the professional code itself should apply if decisions are to be made responsibly.

Another argument bearing on the justification of the principle of full advocacy involves the equitable distribution of legal expertise. If justice is to be served, all should have equal access to the services of a lawyer. Setting aside the question of the varying ability of clients to afford legal services, equal access is presumably the best basis for insuring that cases are decided on their merits—that is, that they are settled justly. In the case of judges, the legal system is dependent upon members of the bench applying the law as it exists. One could claim that the same principle applies to lawyers, since an unequal distribution of legal services will result unless lawyers provide every advantage to a client allowed under the law. While inequality of legal competence among lawyers may be an intractable fact, deprivation of adequate legal counsel through the moral discrimination of lawyers can at least be avoided, under this argument, by compliance with the principle of full advocacy. Without it, clients whom lawyers disliked or disapproved of would not be fairly represented. The operation of the principle thus provides the fairest distribution of legal resources.

This position, however, is not convincing. Lawyers function as individuals rather than as undifferentiated parts of an institutional monolith. If a client believes that the lawyer will not serve his other interests as desired, he or she can seek another. Such is hardly the case with a judge. Thus, if a lawyer informs a client that the lawyer's actions will be limited by certain moral considerations, and the client believes that the lawyer, as a result, will not serve the client's interests, the client can seek legal representation elsewhere. Because legal assistance will still be available even though lawyers do apply general moral criteria to professional decisions, this consideration does not support the argument that the professional function requires full differentiation. One might object that *all* lawyers might refuse their services, but if such were the case, surely it would be overwhelming *prima facie* evidence, considering the variety of moral perspective among lawyers, that support of the client's objectives could not be justified in any coherent rationale. We can conclude from this argument that lawyers should not be prevented by their ethical code from denying their services to a client when they think that pursuit of the prospective client's objectives would be patently unjust or immoral.

Moreover, if lawyers employ the tactics permissible under the full advocacy principle as traditionally interpreted, which not only permits but requires undertaking legal yet immoral actions that further the interests of the client, it appears that the issue of deciding cases on merit is subordinated—in which case the fundamental purpose of achieving justice is not fulfilled. It may be argued that it is the court as a whole that has the responsibility of deciding the merits of a case, and that lawyers best contribute to this by presenting the most effective argument possible for their clients. However, Goldman argues that this is difficult to maintain when one recognizes that the extreme legal tactics not only permissible but required under a full differentiation view serve in many cases to obscure the truth through deception, concealment, and clearly immoral actions.

The reasons for qualifying the principle of full advocacy are strong. There are other arguments against the moral acceptability of full advocacy, and some similar ones for modifying the principle of confidentiality for lawyers. The conclusion strongly suggested is that although the legal profession sometimes appears to assume a fully differentiated role, analysis reveals that only a partially differentiated role can be justified.

The point of Goldman's argument is not that there are some actions allowable under the professional ethic which, from a moral point of view, no lawyer should perform. The point is that functional requirements alone do not require full differentiation in the lawyer's role. There is room within the necessities of functional considerations for adherence to moral standards not included in the codified ethic of the legal profession itself. Goldman argues that lawyers should not be required to follow the ethic literally and specifically in all cases. To do so, in his view, leads to results contrary to the values commonly held to justify the ethic of the legal profession—the values of American society. His quarrel is with the way the legal ethic is currently applied; my concern is not with whether he is right about legal ethics, but with the pattern of analysis that he employs.

In a sense analogous to the situation of lawyers as analyzed by Goldman, the refusal to carry out certain activities on moral grounds, while undoubtedly having traumatic effects on a military professional's career, would normally result in responsibility being shifted to another individual (since the military is a vertically organized institution with an explicit hierarchy of command). Only in the most unusual situations would such a refusal have a crippling effect on the military function, and the question of full differentiation cannot be settled on the basis of such extraordinary and unlikely scenarios. In another consideration suggested by the comparison with lawyers, we can see that actions by the armed forces on behalf of their client can be very harmful to individuals, both citizens and noncitizens. If full differentiation is not functionally necessary in a clearly demonstrable way, and if it may in addition work to the detriment of achieving the moral end served by the profession, claiming such a status appears quite dubious when the moral end is protection of individual integrity and autonomy.

As I noted earlier, the decisions of a judge materially affect the law and establish a precedent that has a formalized impact on subsequent judicial proceedings. No such formalized effect results from the military professional considering moral factors other than the PME alone. Goldman argues that the fallibility of human judgment makes it necessary for judges to follow the rule of law exclusively. To interpose their personal moral views would render the administration of law unpredictable and to some extent arbitrary. Under such conditions, the institution of law would no longer be capable of promoting justice and stability.

Fallibility works in reverse in the military situation, however, because of the separation of military function and moral end. All decisions are subject to human fallibility. If the individual officer errs in applying his moral judgment, the organizational hierarchy ensures that the military function can continue. But if there is no corrective within the chain of command—that is, if the total obedience of full differentiation ruled—grave moral errors could be endlessly and disastrously propagated. Total obedience would render correction of any fallacious judgment impossible. The interests and moral ends of society could themselves be critically endangered from within by one wrong high-level decision. Precisely because of human fallibility, the moral judgment of each individual military officer must act as a check on the military system if the rights of members of American society are ultimately to be protected.

The third of the four factors that appear to support full differentiation involves necessity. If the operation of military necessity were held to override all other considerations, as it was in the German doctrine of *Kriegsraison geht vor Kriegsmanier*,[17] the moral ends served by maintaining the military security of the United States could themselves be endangered. The principle of proportionality, accepted in any moral evaluation of actions in war, requires that the means employed in warfare be proportional to the military ends or objectives involved. Unqualified application of that principle, however, becomes a utilitarian calculation. If the military objective is given an extremely high value (unlimited, perhaps, if the stakes are national survival), then essentially any means can be justified. Even if limited by the laws of war, such a principle makes concern about persons, including the moral rights of individuals, subordinate to utilities. That result clearly subverts the fundamental values of American society which the military exists to serve. As Goldman said of lawyers, the defense of moral autonomy and the rights of the individual cannot extend to the systematic invasion of the proper domain of individual sovereignty. The emphasis here should be on "systematic." To say that military necessity overrides other moral factors is to establish such a systematic invasion in the functioning of the military. Accordingly, the principle of military necessity must itself be subject to the moral judgment of the military professional. In many situations where decisions concerning actions must be made, the military professional alone is in a position to make such judgment.

The fourth feature suggesting full differentiation noted before is also questionable. The obligation to adhere to the laws of war is clear, but the laws of war are fundamentally a means of moral enforcement — a means of implementing certain moral principles. While compliance with the laws of war is indeed a duty for members of the military, all such laws are subject to review under the moral criteria that are now recognized. If the law in particular situations does not serve the moral purposes of the law, a basis exists for applying independent moral judgment or the criteria of "ordinary morality." Military professionals are well prepared to apply such judgment because of their extensive formal education and experience. As they attain positions of greater responsibility and their decisions have broader ramifications, their education and experience progress accordingly.

The case against full differentiation for the role of the military professional is at least as persuasive as the case against full differentiation for lawyers. Nonetheless, the moral aspects of the professional's role call for special weight to be given to the norms of the profession. At least three categories of actions show this to be true, and they are distinguished by the persons whose moral rights are overridden. One category covers those involved in personal relationships with the professional. Moral obligations to both family and friends that would normally be ultimate reasons for action are subordinated to the demands of duty. A second category involves the status of members of the armed forces with respect to civil rights. Rights such as those of free speech and personal liberty which would require recognition and deference from a general moral perspective are in certain situations subordinated by military authorities on the basis of the requirements of the PME. Such subordination normally falls under the operation of the duty principle. The third category concerns various classes of persons outside the parent society—most particularly, hostile combatants and citizens of the state with which the United States is at war. Members of hostile armed forces in war can be attacked and killed even though they present no immediate or direct threat to the offensive force. The uniformed members of a quartermaster unit that repairs tents are legitimate targets of attack for the military, even though the use of lethal force against such a target would obviously be morally unacceptable for anyone other than a combatant in the circumstances of war. "Scorched earth" methods ordered by a retreating military commander which call for the destruction of private property also involve this third category of actions. The property rights of citizens could not justifiably be overridden in such a manner by anyone outside the military role in comparable circumstances. The norms governing role conduct thus result in differentiation from the conduct otherwise acceptable under the values and moral standards of American society (and Western society in general).

To summarize, the military professional, in the preparation for and conduct of war, appropriately takes actions that would be morally impermissible outside the role. The function of the military would not be possible otherwise. Because of their special responsibility to society, however, military professionals must consider and weigh the significance of their actions in terms of the general moral principles which derive from the basic values of society. While fundamental American values have shaped the PME, the content of the American PME as discussed in chapter 4 does not deal directly with the broad concepts of freedom and equality that are so central to the American value system. And of course no code of principles attempts to eliminate the use of judgment by those governed by it. When individual moral rights are subordinated, the rationally consistent justification must ultimately be in terms of the fundamental values of society. If the foundational values of self-determination and individual personality appear to be subverted by specific alternatives, officers must weigh their special obligations as professionals and their functional requirements against the violation of individual moral rights. That constitutes what has been described previously as partial differentiation. Thus, in a partially differentiated role and in applying an ethical code that reflects such partial differentiation, two sets of somewhat differing moral rules must be employed to choose among morally significant actions. This partial differentiation differs from that of the lawyer in that the limitations on conduct are ultimately determined not by functional requirements, but by moral principles independent of the professional function. If professional decisions involving moral issues are to be made consistently, the issue that must be settled is the relationship between the two sets of moral considerations: the PME and the fundamental values of society.

Fulfilling the responsibilities of a partially differentiated role can obviously be quite difficult. Succinct, absolute norms simplify the moral universe. In a role in which such an analysis shifts toward consequences cumulatively "best" and unattainable through even well-intentioned judgment, full differentiation can perhaps be justified in teleological terms. But in the case of the military professional, simplification would create an unacceptable threat to the very values that the American military exists to protect. Further, full differentiation is not clearly essential to the function of the military professional, while partial role differentiation is. If the military is to endure as a profession, it must have, in applying force, the moral authority to take those actions necessary to defend American society against threats to its continued existence. The responsibility for wielding such authority appropriately places a severe demand upon the judgment of the American soldier in his or her function as the defender of a free society—and that is precisely why the role of the military careerist should be that of a full-fledged military professional insofar as commitment and competence are concerned.

The relationship between the boundary conditions and the PME can be compared to the relationship between the rules of a particular kind of athletic contest and the norms of society. The participants in the contest have an objective: establishing the conditions under which one contestant can be said to have won. The rules of the game are focused on the appropriate means of accomplishing that end.

However, the rules must themselves be consistent with the norms of society, for in our peculiar contest, the winner is to exemplify the normative standards of society. If those standards and the means of achieving victory were inconsistent, the significance of the contest would be lost. In such a case, the norms of society are not formally part of the rules, but they are integral to the contest because they have shaped the nature of such rules and they also establish limits on what the rules can require.

In a similar sense, the values of American society as such are not part of the PME, but they establish limitations within which the prescriptions of the PME necessarily fall (if they are to be consistent). If all values of American society were actually part of the PME, the PME would indeed be fully differentiated in a trivial sense (one would follow *only* the PME in making moral choices), and our only concerns would be articulating the PME and maintaining internal consistency. That, however, is not the nature of our model, which differentiates roles within the context of a particular society regarding conduct permissible under the moral standards and values of the society. To the limiting relationship between the PME and the values of American society, we can apply the term "boundary condition." The boundary-condition relationship is particularly significant with respect to the duty principle.

The Duty Principle

Without some further clarification, the broad principles of the American PME which were articulated in chapter 4 could conflict with each other. They could also dictate actions that appear inconsistent with fundamental American values. Both results would tend toward moral incoherence and logical inconsistency, and the latter result would make it difficult to argue that the PME is rationally justifiable in the context of American society. Certain conditions for applying the principles—what I have referred to as boundary conditions—are necessary to avoid such consequences.

The principles of the uncodified PME are subject to these boundary conditions. As I have described them in this discussion, the principles state that professional soldiers:

1. Accept service to country as their watchword and defense of the Constitution of the United States of America as their calling.
2. Place their duty first. They subordinate their personal interests to the requirements of their professional functions.
3. Conduct themselves at all times as persons of honor whose integrity, loyalty, and courage are exemplary. Such qualities are essential on the battlefield if a military organization is to function effectively.
4. Develop and maintain the highest possible level of professional knowledge and skill. To do less is to fail to meet their obligations to the country, the profession, and fellow soldiers.
5. Take full responsibility for the manner in which their orders are carried out.
6. Promote and safeguard, within the context of mission accomplishment, the welfare of their subordinates as persons, not merely as soldiers.
7. Conform strictly to the principle that subordinates the military to civilian authority. They do not involve themselves or their subordinates in domestic politics beyond the exercise of basic civil rights.
8. Adhere to the laws of war and the regulations of their service in performing their professional functions.

Conflict among these principles is obviously possible, but the resolution of some of the apparent differences is not difficult insofar as the priority of the principles is concerned. If, for example, the requirements of a particular mission, itself reasonably conceived, are detrimental to the welfare of the individual soldier, the duty of mission accomplishment is to be given prior consideration. The most compelling requirements of duty are those actions necessary in the preservation and furtherance of the security of the state under the Constitution. In many actual instances, duty will in fact be reduced at lower echelons to obedience to orders, for the connection of specific actions to the security of the state will not be clear. These are the situations which can become agonizing for individuals, but the relationship between the principles is not in question.

Equating duty with obedience to orders is a common but serious failing of the officer corps. Though duty prevails for the military professional, obedience to orders may be questionable when strong evidence exists that certain actions will *not* be in the interests of the security of the state. Such questioning is itself based upon the requirements of the duty principle, because duty for the American military professional is not simply a commitment to subordinate personal and other interests to those of national security. The commitment of the American military officer is to maintain a particular value structure within American society. "Support and defense of the Constitution requires fealty to the principles, to the values, proclaimed by that document."[18] The duty principle, in the American PME, is thus considerably broader than it would be if it were determined by the functional requirements of military activity alone.[19]

Another type of situation sometimes considered problematic is that in which the duty to preserve the security of the state appears to conflict with the principle of subordination to civilian authority. The duty to preserve the state, however, is that of preserving the security of the state *under the Constitution*. And "under the Constitution" limits the military's responsibilities to those designated by civilian authority. So long as the civilian authorities act within the legal limits established by the Constitution and municipal law, there is no question concerning the relationship between these two principles. The duty of the military professional is to preserve (and thus inherently to accept) the authority of the civilian leadership as a fundamental aspect of the security of the state.

By relating these principles to the principle of duty in brief, I do not intend to minimize the complex problem of determining precisely what one's duty consists of in the shifting, dimly comprehended circumstances of actual situations. Even when the facts of a situation are clear, moral choice may demand more moral courage than even a competent professional can muster, as our various case studies indicate.

Some difficulties as well cannot be dealt with in such encompassing terms. Those that are of particular concern again center on the duty principle. Its role in the PME is central in the same manner that the principle of full advocacy is central in the legal code: if the principle is based on functional requirements alone, it becomes the basis for arguing for the status of full differentiation. In the case of lawyers, if full advocacy as stated in the *Code of Professional Responsibility* is accepted without qualification, it follows that the role is fully differentiated. In the case of military officers, if the duty principle as stated here is restricted to functional considerations alone, full differentiation appears to be indicated. The rationale for justification in both instances begins with the claim that full differentiation is necessary if the profession is to achieve its primary purpose. If we conclude, as we have, that full differentiation is neither necessary nor justifiable, the question becomes how the duty principle is to be modified. What are the boundary conditions that allow the duty principle to facilitate the professional function, but that do not permit the principle to be used to justify every alternative presented by military necessity and proportionality?[20]

Part of the answer emerged in chapter 5. The laws of war, under the seventh provision of the PME, establish specific limitations, but the laws are both incomplete and changing. Their content is a result of a process of evolution and compromise. Quite simply, the laws of war alone do not render the PME consistent and coherent in application. In any particular case covered by the laws of war, however, members of the American military are constrained in their actions by the laws. In addition, the principle of duty is constrained by the fundamental values of American society. Three sets of boundary conditions for morally permissible conduct thus exist, with the functional requirements of military activity—military necessity, if you will—being the most inclusive in terms of allowable actions. The laws of war, as a second set of boundary conditions, narrow the spectrum of allowable actions further, and the third set—the fundamental values of American society—will in most cases restrict permissible actions even more.

The type of case in which issues of morally permissible conduct are most evident is the kind of situation in which actions that are apparently dictated by assigned missions (such as those essential to the critical interests of American society) appear to be in conflict with the rights of a person or group. The fundamental values of freedom, equality, democracy, and individualism will establish limitations on the actions morally permissible under the duty principle, if that principle is to be justifiable in terms of those fundamental values.

A rather dramatic hypothetical case illustrates the difficulty of the choice between national interests and individual rights. Variations of the following scenario have been discussed frequently in recent years. A foreign agent has been captured by the military. Available evidence suggests that the agent knows the location of an atomic weapon hidden in Washington, D.C.—a weapon known to be set to explode within a short time. The time is insufficient to warn the civilian authorities and convince them of the accuracy of the report, let alone to evacuate the capital. The security of the state appears to be seriously threatened (though disillusioned observers may debate the extent of damage that might occur in terms of national leadership). If the officer in charge believes that the situation is as described, is he or she justified in using all possible methods to make the captured agent reveal the location of the weapon? If such revelation could prevent the explosion of the bomb, is the officer permitted to torture the prisoner? Is the officer justified in threatening and then performing the torture or execution of innocent persons important to the agent if that will persuade the agent to reveal the location?

The question of torture is hardly new. Today, the stakes are simply potentially greater. One could argue that the attempt to destroy a large segment of the population of Washington is a sufficient basis for claiming that the agent has forfeited the right to be treated as a person. For our purposes, however, we will assume that torture is generally morally impermissible under the common norms of morality. Even so, the question remains as to what the officer in charge should do. The officer has a particular duty to preserve and further the security of the state. That duty goes beyond the moral obligation of any person to prevent significant harm to others if such prevention were in his or her power and could be achieved without harm to self or others. The professional officer has made a specific moral commitment and has a more extensive responsibility. In this hypothetical situation, if torturing the prisoner will prevent the explosion of the weapon, the result will be fewer violations of fundamental moral rights than if the action had not been taken. In addition, the security of the state will apparently have been enhanced.

While an individual person as such might not be morally justified in torturing the agent, the officer in charge wields the authority of the state. He or she has the power and the responsibility to employ violence in protecting state interests. If we were to assume that the state will no longer exist if the weapon explodes (dubious though that assumption is), the issue of necessity comes into play. One might be tempted to say that the soldier then has the authority and the responsibility to take action that would not be appropriate for a general member of the society.

While fundamental rights are those that cannot be overridden by the aggregation of lesser interests over a number of persons, the rights involved in this case are equally important. In question are the rights of both the agent and the people of Washington to life and to freedom from suffering purposely inflicted by others. Without question, fewer such rights will be violated if the agent is tortured and the population spared. If rights are in some sense commensurable, if we can compare them and assign weights to the elements compared, we can readily resolve the situation.

If one concludes that, within the context of American society, torture is justified in such a case (which is to say that torture is, at a minimum, morally permissible in certain circumstances), a principle appears to have been invoked. Despite the focus on rights, the principle is consequentialist and quite familiar: the results of the action justify the means employed, at least in these extreme cases. While we are usually reluctant to concede the acceptability of the consequentialist or utilitarian position if the stakes are lower, our moral convictions often appear to undergo a transformation when national survival is at stake.[21]

Such a transformation, however, would render our moral position inconsistent. In the most obvious rationalization, nationalism would seem to be granted the highest priority among the values of American society. But our previous discussion suggests strongly that this is not the case. As one eminent critic pointed out, "[A democratic society] is itself required to respect the individual's autonomy and liberty, and in general to treat him justly."[22] Otherwise, the society is no longer one characterized by the values we profess.

If the value of individual personality and the consequent principles hold, numbers do not dictate a change in application. Thus, an argument based on human suffering will not provide justification either. If rights are derived from the intrinsic worth of persons, then they are not additive across persons. The equivalent rights of five people are not to be weighed more heavily than the same right of one person on the basis of numbers alone. If it is morally wrong to sacrifice one person for another because of what it means to be a person, it must also be morally wrong to sacrifice one person against his or her will for fifty thousand others. To conclude otherwise is to resort to a form of consequentialist calculation. And while some might argue for just such reasoning, to do so would be to depart from the fundamental moral concepts professed by American society.[23]

If the officer in charge does take action to force the agent to provide information, we may well excuse that action to some degree; that is, we may find the actions to be less blameworthy than they would be in other circumstances, but we will not be able to justify them. We will not be able to say, without qualification, that torture of the terrorist or those involved with the terrorist was the morally right thing to do.

In essence, neither the American PME nor the American value system is consequentialist in nature. Within the context of American values, torture and other uses of persons solely as means are not morally permissible. The officer in charge in our hypothetical bomb case may decide to torture the prisoner, but he or she cannot claim moral justification in terms of the American value system. The actions may be morally excused to some degree, but they cannot be justified. Those who would claim that they can must argue a case that reduces to justifying the violation of individual rights on the basis of benefits to many. While such arguments are familiar and often plausible in various guises, they are not sufficient for the American value system — nor for any moral system in which the individual is recognized as having intrinsic worth and as possessing fundamental moral rights that can be justly overridden only on the basis of a principle such as that of greatest equal liberty.[24] This conclusion can also be reached in another manner. If professional exigencies alone are considered, the values of the military perspective indicate that whatever action is necessary to preserve the state or to minimize injury to it should be taken. The value of nationalism in the military perspective certainly could be considered as a sufficient basis for an ultimate justifying reason. That this is not the case in the American PME is significant. The modification of the military viewpoint is the result of the value system of American society. In that system, as we discussed in chapter 6, nationalism is instrumental in terms of moral ends rather than being an end in itself. Accordingly, morally permissible actions under the duty principle of the American PME are limited by considerations arising from the American value system. We concluded previously that one of the humanitarian principles underlying the laws of war, which states that individual persons are to be respected as such, was also operative under the American value system. This principle is an important element in the laws of war that protect human rights, including the right not to be tortured. The laws do not allow the mistreatment of any persons under military control, whether soldiers or civilians, spies or saboteurs, terrorists or murderers.

The same restrictions apply to the military in any professional function. In any armed conflict or state uses of military force, the military is restricted by the laws of war and the principles underlying them. Torture is obviously not permissible under this consideration. Because the humanitarian principle can also be derived from the American value system, in parallel fashion torture is morally impermissible as a result of the boundary conditions for the application of the American PME.

The final boundary conditions are the set of fundamental American values. It provides the answer to the question, "What factors, after consideration of the PME itself, limit what can be done to achieve successful mission accomplishment?" Actions required under the duty principle are limited to those that are consistent with the American value system—meaning that actions taken under the PME are morally permissible only if they do not subvert or controvert the fundamental moral values of American society. Such a conclusion denies a consequentialist basis for the *moral* aspects of professional decisions. The PME functions under a moral teleology, but the purpose of the PME is to guide the efforts of the military to maintain the state under the Constitution. The purpose is to uphold a matrix of institutional values. To provide consistent guidance, the PME cannot approve actions which conflict morally with that set of values.

As a result of the boundary conditions established by the American value system, authoritarianism—one of the functional tendencies of military activity—is also limited. The American PME traditionally has not accepted or condoned stereotypical obedience to orders, even though indoctrination and particular practices may sometimes suggest the opposite. Within the context of tactical actions on the battlefield, immediate and reflexive response to orders is indeed the objective of some military training, because it makes a military unit more effective in the overwhelming confusion of stress of combat. Such training, however, does not abrogate the individual's responsibility to refuse to obey illegal orders.

Does that requirement place individual soldiers in situations that they may perceive as moral dilemmas? It may, but the policy of insisting on individual responsibility remains morally necessary. Situations do occur in which privates must act and in acting apparently choose between risk to themselves and their units, on the one hand, and risk to unarmed noncombatants on the other. Flag officers sometimes face the decision whether to issue orders that are not only necessary to make success in war possible but that also endanger the lives and welfare of civilian populations. Throughout the spectrum, from individual soldier to theater commander, members of the military must choose and act knowing that life and death hang in the balance.

No set of rules can provide answers in every case or even in most. We can only seek to understand the applicable moral principles clearly, weigh our experience and our responsibilities, and determine which course of action is most defensible. Long after traumatic events such as the bombing of Hiroshima and Nagasaki, despite years of analysis and debate, we are often unable to reach a moral consensus. In the sphere of combat, however, as death and human disaster hammer the senses, time for reflection is seldom available: the person in uniform must choose a course of action. Because so much hangs in the balance so often, war is indeed the hardest place to maintain our humanity.

Chapter Eight

The Rubber and the Road: Case Studies

As a form of commentary as well as practical application, I offer a set of case studies that present difficult choices. The conclusions I draw are subject to debate. Nonetheless, I do want to maintain two points: (1) the process of moral analysis suggested here is appropriate for such cases, including "the hardest place," and (2) for a military professional, moral judgment is unavoidable.

In each of the discussions that follow, I examine the circumstances relative to the American PME. Where necessary, I invoke the boundary conditions to clarify the conceptual issues and moral considerations involved in identifying a resolution justifiable in the model of moral analysis I have discussed. When the morally preferable choice is not clear in a situation, one should examine the alternatives in terms of the boundary conditions that structure the American PME.

Case 1: The Operations Officer

Situation

Captain Green is an operations officer of an infantry battalion serving with American forces in the Vietnam War. His battalion has been fighting intense but brief battles with enemy units on the northern edge of the Mekong Delta. The unit is protecting the capital city of Saigon by blocking routes to the city from the southwest and attacking enemy forces in the area.

The southern part of the battalion's area of operations has been declared a "free fire zone" under the rules of engagement, which means that all persons considered friendly to the Vietnamese government have been evacuated. Any persons remaining in the zone are to be considered enemy and can be fired on if it has been established that no friendly military activity is under way in the zone.

The method of operation employed by Captain Green's battalion is that of occupying patrol bases of company and platoon size to block any movement toward Saigon. Frequently, the battalion consolidates and conducts heliborne operations against enemy concentrations. The battalion is about to conduct such an assault. The infantry units are in the air aboard helicopters, and Captain Green, along with the battalion commander and other staff officers, is in a command and control helicopter above the landing zone (LZ) that the battalion will use. Since it is outside the supporting artillery range, the LZ is being fired upon by armed helicopters before the landing in order to eliminate or suppress potential enemy resistance, though no enemy forces have been observed in the vicinity. Following his established pattern for such operations, the battalion commander gives his orders to Captain Green, who then uses the helicopter's communications systems to coordinate execution.

The battalion commander has been intently observing a small village about four hundred meters from the area where the helicopters will land. Helicopter assaults are seldom conducted outside the range of supporting artillery, and the battalion commander is uneasy about the risk involved should significant resistance be met during the landing. The LZ and the village are just north of the free fire zone, so the operation has been carefully coordinated with the Vietnamese district chief who controls this area. Any fires delivered in the district other than in situations of self-defense requiring immediate return fire must be approved by the district headquarters. The village causing the battalion commander concern has not been fired upon during the LZ preparation by the armed helicopters.

The battalion commander turns to Captain Green and asks if the village is outside the area cleared by the district headquarters for the LZ preparation. Captain Green replies that it seems to be right at the edge according to his map overlay. The battalion commander directs Captain Green to have the armed helicopters hit the village with rockets and machine gun fire as the landing begins. He suspects some automatic weapons may be emplaced in the village which could fire on the lift helicopters as they land. Captain Green points out that they have seen women and children running to what appear to be earthen shelters in the village during the LZ preparation, but the battalion commander is firm: he wants the village taken under fire.

Captain Green is struck by indecision. He has no inclination to disobey his commander's order—quite the contrary. At the same time, he recognizes that firing on the village will almost certainly cause injuries among seeming noncombatants. Further, the rules of engagement in this area preclude firing into built-up areas without coordination and prior approval unless such action is immediately necessary in self-defense.

Discussion

Captain Green has a duty to obey his commander—a stringent duty absolutely essential to efficient military operations—but he also has a duty to disobey illegal orders. He must decide whether the order he has received is illegal. If there are enemy forces in the village that directly threaten the battalion, firing at those forces is a legal act. If it is known that some noncombatants are in the immediate vicinity of the enemy positions and the enemy fire immediately endangers one's own soldiers, returning fire is still permissible under the rules of engagement. Assuming that the intent is to save one's own unit, unintentional injury or loss of life among noncombatants is one of the tragedies of war. Responsibility for the injury to noncombatants rests primarily with the enemy force that failed to remove them. While the noncombatant casualties would be highly regrettable, the life-threatening situation and the mission would justify firing in defense. If no life-threatening situation exists, however, the order to fire upon the village is illegal as well as immoral.

Military necessity is sometimes cited in defense of acts that constitute willful killing of noncombatants, who qualify as "protected persons" under the Geneva Conventions. If firing on the village caused the injury or death of noncombatants, it would certainly appear to be willful and to fall under the prohibitions of the 1949 Geneva Conventions (Geneva Convention Relative to the Protection of Civilian Persons in Time of War, Article 147). In this case, there seems to be no basis for claiming military necessity.

Situation Continued

Captain Green tells the battalion commander that they should seek approval from the district headquarters since no enemy elements are actually known to be there. The battalion commander decides to refrain for the time being. Moments later, however, one of the armed helicopter pilots reports that he has received automatic weapons fire from the village and requests permission to initiate suppressive fires. The battalion commander tells Captain Green to "take care of it." Captain Green again finds himself uncertain.

Discussion Continued

Captain Green recognizes that firing on the village will almost certainly cause noncombatant casualties. He should also recognize that the situation is not directly life-threatening. Immediate suppressive fires are not obviously justifiable. Both the size of the enemy force and the number of noncombatants in the village are unknown. Captain Green also remembers that in any case, under the rules of engagement, built-up areas are not to be fired upon except in self-defense without approval from higher headquarters. The act of firing upon the village in these circumstances would be unauthorized and thus unjustifiable under the existing rules of engagement established by the American military command. Captain Green also knows that the helicopter assault can be redirected to an alternate LZ. His logical course of action is to recommend to the battalion commander that the incoming lift helicopters be rerouted to an alternate LZ. To provide flexibility as the situation develops, he may also want to initiate a request to the district headquarters to fire upon the village.

Firing on the village in an attempt to eliminate the enemy threat, knowing that noncombatants would be as likely to be injured as the enemy, could be justified only if failure to do so would immediately endanger the lives or critical resources of American forces. That would be the case even if the technicality of obtaining the district chief's permission to fire had already been met. It would be true as well if noncombatants had been identified in a similar situation in the free fire zone to the south.

The limitations of Captain Green's alternatives are both legal and moral. While the moral innocence of those identified as noncombatants is sometimes problematic, even the most basic respect for persons requires that the presumption of innocence be extended to those who appear to fall into the category of noncombatants. To do otherwise would clearly contravene the fundamental American values of freedom and individuality. Such violation would mean that the application of the PME—if it were considered to condone or require an action which involved denial of the presumption of innocence—was not limited by the set of fundamental social values. A PME that is not so limited is not a justifiable PME in the context of the American society which our military serves.

Case 2: The Brigade Commander

Situation

Colonel Red is the commander of an infantry brigade in Vietnam. The year is 1968, shortly after the Tet Offensive. Colonel Red's brigade is assigned a large area of operations within which he is to destroy both main force enemy units and the Viet Cong (VC) infrastructure.

Since the Tet Offensive, the American command in Saigon has been under intense pressure to produce positive results and thereby to demonstrate that the battle against the VC and the North Vietnamese is being won. Colonel Red's division commander has informed his subordinate commanders that while vital U.S. national interests are at stake in Vietnam, Congress is being pushed by public sentiment to require withdrawal of U.S. forces. That sentiment, he believes, is fueled by both communist propaganda and a perception that the American military effort is nonproductive and futile. Higher command and the current administration each contend that public opinion is dangerously misguided. The division commander has repeatedly emphasized that it is vital to achieve a record of successful operations against the enemy during the current period of doubt at home.

With these points in mind, Colonel Red finds himself in a dilemma. He has just finished sitting in on a briefing presented by the division commander to the commander of all American forces in Vietnam (COMUSMACV). The division commander has told COMUSMACV that in an operation which Colonel Red's brigade has just completed—one resulting in heavy casualties to one of Colonel Red's battalions—over four hundred enemy soldiers were killed. Earlier in the day, Colonel Red, having joined his engaged forces toward the end of the battle and having walked the area and talked after the engagement with the units involved, had briefed the division commander on the details of the operation. Colonel Red had told him that only forty enemy bodies were found, though supporting artillery and air bombardment of the enemy had been heavy. Since Colonel Red's companies had suffered over one hundred fifty casualties, including fifty-three dead, the verifiable "kill ratio" had been quite unfavorable even though the enemy unit had been driven from the area. The figures reported by the division commander to COMUSMACV in the afternoon briefing were patently false.

Colonel Red is a career army officer. He has private doubts about the effectiveness of current U.S. combat operations in Vietnam, but the most effective remedy in his view is an extension of the ground war into North Vietnam and Laos, which provide essentially secure bases for operations against the American and South Vietnamese forces. As Colonel Red sees it, the North Vietnamese enjoy all the strategic offensive options, while the American and South Vietnamese forces remain restricted to a strategic defensive posture. Colonel Red accepts the importance of the U.S. role in the Vietnamese struggle, believing that the fall of the South Vietnamese government would be unacceptable in terms of U.S. interests. As a military professional, Colonel Red is not sure what he should do in this instance. He recognizes his duty to be loyal to his commander and to do all he can to bring about the success of the overall mission.

Discussion

Colonel Red has a professional responsibility to report truthfully. He has done so. However, the purpose of truthful reporting in a military context is in large part provided by the need for accurate information in making responsible decisions. Superiors will hardly make effective decisions concerning the application of force and the use of resources if the decisions are based upon false or inaccurate data. Colonel Red knows that the division commander's report is inaccurate. He should also recognize that the objective act of false reporting is morally wrong in itself, though the wrongness could be ameliorated by the subjective factor of intent.

Colonel Red has a number of options. Among them:

1. He can keep silent and do his own job to the best of his ability.
2. He can keep silent but request a transfer out of the division.
3. He can discuss the matter with the division commander and express his views.
4. He can attempt to correct the false report.
5. He can resign his commission in protest and publicize his reasons.

This set of alternatives presents Colonel Red with a difficult choice. If he decides to keep silent and continue carrying out the immediate responsibilities of his command position, he recognizes that the false report of which he is aware will probably be uncorrected. His unit will certainly hear of the inflated casualty report. Many soldiers, privy to only a small part of the battle, may assume that actions of which they were unaware produced the enemy casualties. A number will know, however, that the figures are drastically inflated. Colonel Red realizes that a logical conclusion will be that he himself is the source of the erroneous reporting. If that perception were to become widespread, Colonel Red's integrity in the eyes of his command would be severely tarnished. The most obvious interpretation of such an action would be one which categorized Colonel Red as a highly ambitious and apparently unprincipled officer seeking to protect and enhance his own reputation. Besides undermining his effectiveness, such a result would also feed the inevitable cynicism about "higher headquarters." This series of events would clearly be undesirable.

Any attempt to inform his command of the source of the false report would only make matters worse. It would only be natural for some of his subordinates to question Colonel Red's word, and shifting responsibility one level higher would hardly moderate a cynical response. Colonel Red is also concerned about the effect on future reporting by his unit that the false casualty figures may produce. The principle of truth-telling is obviously weakened if soldiers perceive that higher headquarters is going to alter statistics for its own purposes regardless of the reports received. They may conclude that falsification of their own reports is expected.

The second alternative—keeping silent but requesting a transfer—is obviously not a viable solution. While it might remove Colonel Red from a difficult position in one sense, the problems of principle would remain for the division and the army, which is Colonel Red's primary concern from a professional point of view. While one false report will, in itself, hardly affect major strategic or even significant tactical decisions, a pattern of false reporting would be a serious failing that could lead to misinformed decisions of great consequence. The effects on the soldiers and professionals under Colonel Red's command could also be telling in the long run, conceivably even to the extent of undermining the entire American effort to assist the South Vietnamese government.

The third alternative—discussing the matter with the division commander—will be personally difficult. While it may reveal some logical reason for the false report, it will probably result in the division commander's animosity. He may tell Colonel Red that the reason for the greatly inflated figures on enemy casualties is a determination to deny ammunition to those who misguidedly seek to curtail American military involvement in Vietnam. While such an intent might be understandable, it would hardly be supportable in Colonel Red's view. The army's responsibility is to carry out assigned missions and to provide accurate professional reporting, analysis, and evaluation to superiors, not to determine national policy decisions. If the division commander were motivated in some sense such as this, he would be advocating the substitution of the military's view of what was best for the country for that of the civilian leadership and society in general.

The division commander might also direct Colonel Red to leave such matters to him and run his own brigade. On the other hand, he might decide to avoid such incidents in the future if he knew that Colonel Red was strongly opposed on principle to his actions. If the division commander condones violations of the principle of truth-telling for reasons of expediency, and simply misjudged how Colonel Red would react, a serious problem would remain. Colonel Red should recognize that the division commander is high enough in the military hierarchy to provide a far-reaching and deleterious example if he does not adhere to the principle of truth-telling. Further, he is in a position to "contaminate" the information upon which significant tactical decisions are made.

If Colonel Red attempts to correct the false report outside the regular channel through division headquarters, he will be violating the principle of loyalty in a dramatic fashion. Such an effort may result in controversy and doubt rather than clarification. In any case, it would probably be disastrous for Colonel Red's career. Though he should recognize that as a personal rather than a strictly professional interest, it is a consideration that would nonetheless loom large in anyone's mind. However his attempt to correct the record turned out, his motives would be misinterpreted and his judgment severely questioned. Most professionals at a distance, firmly convinced of the necessity for loyalty in military organizations, would conclude that there must have been more appropriate ways to handle such a situation.

The last alternative—to resign in protest and make the reasons known—is a traditionally accepted response to policies or orders of superiors that are unacceptable to the individual professional. Weighing against this choice is the possibility of misinterpretation, which can obscure the purpose of the act of resignation. Colonel Red realizes that little attention may be given to the resignation of one colonel as a result of what could well be seen as a personality conflict between a subordinate and his superior rather than a resignation on principle.

An additional empirical factor to consider is the extent to which false reporting actually occurs and the extent to which it is tolerated. If it is tolerated, bypassing the division headquarters will not be effective. Transfer to another organization would not even help Colonel Red's personal situation if falsification for command purposes is generally condoned. If the division commander's report is an isolated instance, a discussion with him that reveals Colonel Red's professional concern may be sufficient to rectify the situation, though it will hardly improve relations between Colonel Red and his commander. If the practice is pervasive and is subtly and indirectly condoned, Colonel Red may not be able to find a clear basis for choosing among the alternatives. If such practices are indeed widespread, the officer corps and the society it serves have a serious problem.

The issues in a case such as this, however, revolve about the principle of truth-telling. The duty principle requires that Colonel Red take action in opposing fundamentally misguided decisions by his commander that are clearly detrimental to the protection of national interests. If the difference is one of professional judgment concerning functional requirements, then the superior's views prevail. If the difference involves a violation of professional ethics, however, Colonel Red has an obligation to do what is necessary to uphold the principle of truth-telling. To do so appears to serve not only that principle, but also the principle of subordination to civilian control, the exigencies of the profession, and the national interest.

Case 3: The Company Commander

Situation

Captain White commands an infantry company participating in an antiguerrilla campaign in a small Central American nation. American forces have been committed to combat to help maintain a tottering democratic government, which is opposed by well-organized revolutionary forces that are supported by various states (primarily Cuba). The American forces provide security for sensitive areas in the country, thereby freeing the beleaguered government troops for offensive operations. Captain White's company patrols a sector where small guerrilla forces have raided for some time. The company is part of a network of units securing a large port and logistical center on the coast.

Each day, twenty-one company-sized units involved in security receive a requirement to send out a certain number of patrols and ambushes into designated areas within their sectors of responsibility. In response to these orders, each company submits a plan showing patrol routes and ambush locations to their various battalion headquarters. These are in turn forwarded to the Logistic Support Center Command (LSCC).

The daily routine has gone on for nearly six weeks. Casualties in Captain White's company have been rather high, and most of them have occurred in Area B-7—a reference to a particular portion of the company's sector. The B-7 subsector is an elliptical area with the long axis running north and south, framed by two rivers created when a larger tributary splits into two channels at the north end. The two channels rejoin at the southern point, forming an island three-fourths of a mile wide and two miles long. In the center of the area is a village of perhaps one hundred people who work small plots of land in the vicinity. Each day Captain White receives a requirement to conduct one moving patrol and one ambush patrol within B-7. Time and again, as his units move into the area, they are themselves ambushed or encounter mines and boobytraps. The men in Captain White's company have nicknamed Area B-7 "the Cemetery."

The region in which the company operates is a patchwork of dense jungle and open areas resulting from past efforts at cultivation. Within B-7, the ground is mostly level and open, but along the riverbanks, the growth is impenetrable. There are only two foot routes into B-7: small footbridges on the east and west sides. The approaches to the footbridges are continually boobytrapped, and it is almost impossible to move into the Cemetery undiscovered.

Captain White's security responsibilities are such that he cannot leave a force in B-7 permanently. He is dubious about leaving them there in an isolated position anyway. Helicopter support is infrequent, making reinforcement by air unreliable. All airmobile assets other than medical evacuation are devoted to offensive operations. Captain White has told his commander of his difficulties and requested that the B-7 patrol requirements be dropped. He has used boats on the river in an attempt to find other entrances to B-7, but to no avail. He has talked to the head man in the B-7 village, but the villagers are struggling to remain neutral and to avoid retribution by either side in the conflict, though they always manage to evade boobytrap locations. Captain White suspects that there are guerrillas among the villagers, but he knows that the command policy concerning civilians is extremely strict. The American command is determined to avoid the abuses that occurred on occasion in Vietnam.

The patrols go daily into B-7, and almost every time one or more men are lost. The noncommissioned officers in the company have worked out an informal policy in which each man, after making four patrols into B-7, is assigned to other missions until all men in the unit have made four trips into the Cemetery. The turnover rate has been such that few men have had to make more than the four patrols.

On the previous day, Captain White accompanied one of the patrols into the Cemetery. A boobytrap consisting of a small mortar shell surrounded by crockery killed two men and wounded a third. The device was located about fifty yards from the bridge across the river. Though the patrol's approach had been extremely cautious, with a search for boobytraps and mines, the command-detonated shell was not discovered before it exploded.

Captain White is respected by his men, as are his officers and sergeants. They know that Captain White has gone into B-7 many times. Morale is extremely low, however, and the pressure of the daily patrols against an enemy seldom seen but constantly threatening is taking a severe psychological toll. Captain White recognizes that unless the pattern changes, his men may one day refuse to go into the Cemetery.

The B-7 requirement is one imposed by a distant headquarters that displays no sensitivity to "minor patrolling losses." Captain White's commander is an experienced career soldier whose primary concern is efficiency and mission accomplishment. He appears unwilling to make an issue of B-7 with higher headquarters. In Captain White's assessment, the requirement most probably stems from a staff officer's aversion to asymmetry in the dots on the map reviewed daily at LSCC headquarters. He has come to the conclusion that his men are casualties of bureaucracy and inertia more than enemy action. The losses of the previous day have crystallized his growing misgivings. He believes that further casualties in an apparently senseless mission are intolerable.

A night of intense introspection has revealed several possible actions. The most radical of these is to refuse to send his men into the Cemetery again on routine patrols. Captain White recognizes that such a protest would result in his rapid replacement by another company commander who would, initially at least, continue the B-7 missions. He could also report patrols but simply not send his men out. That possibility, however, is one that Captain White plainly cannot accept. It conflicts with his fundamental view of himself as a professional officer and with the standards of performance that he applies to his conduct. In addition, for technical reasons — including regular infrared and "people sniffer" missions by intelligence elements — such an evasion would soon be detected.

Various alternative techniques of meeting the patrol requirements, such as infiltration and stay-behind patrols, have been tried and failed to solve the difficulty. Restrictions on the use of supporting fires make "firepower solutions" unacceptable. If required to go into B-7, Captain White would prefer to go in behind a wall of artillery fire, but that is not possible in this situation.

After Captain White examines all potential solutions that he has identified, he believes that he is faced with a fundamental choice: either (1) refuse to obey orders, or (2) continue sending men to death and injury for no defensible purpose.

Discussion

In this situation, the PME requirement to perform assigned duties seems to run headlong into the requirement to safeguard the welfare of subordinates. In more general terms, performance of duty appears to conflict with the humanitarian imperative to treat individual persons with respect as such. To continue sending men into a situation in which casualties appear inevitable, for no apparent end other than following orders, is clearly to use them solely as means. In fact, however, low-ranking members of the chain of command seldom know the larger purposes of generals and armies (when there are such purposes), and they are even less frequently in a position to evaluate the requirements and ramifications. Explanation of detailed policy and purpose to the lower operating levels would often mean insufficient responsiveness and the defeat of those policies and purposes. That fact is the reason for the functional requirement of obedience in military activity. Such combat realities are one of the sources of the functional military values of discipline and loyalty. If war is undertaken for apparently just purposes, individuals at operating levels must perform legal orders if those purposes are to be realized. The platoon leader ordered to make a frontal assault on an enemy position that obviously cannot be penetrated by such a force may well believe that lives are being wasted, but he can seldom know whether such an action is not part of a larger series of planned events that will in combination be the wisest and most humane course of action available.

Captain White may be in such a position, but the relevant fact is that he believes he is not. He is sure that the hemorrhaging of his unit is pointless and thus intolerable. He perceives both a moral and a professional obligation to change the course of events. He does not think that it is morally acceptable to continue the patrolling of B-7 in the manner required by his orders.

His first step, regardless of what follows, is to inform his commander of his convictions in the matter. He has already expressed his concern, but now that his doubt has become a firm conviction and a reason for action, the principle of loyalty demands that he make that position known to his commander. It is possible that his response to the situation will trigger some appropriate accommodation. If discussion with his commander produces no results, Captain White is faced with his original choices. The daily patrol requirement makes a rapid decision imperative and unavoidable.

Consideration of the PME itself sheds little light. Upon first reflection, duty requires obedience to legal orders, which are in conflict with considerations of subordinate welfare. Both the performance of duty requirement and the principles of loyalty and truth-telling weigh heavily against any deception such as false reporting of his company's activities. Larger issues of national security, civilian authority, politics, and the laws of war are not relevant to the situation. The moral principles manifested in the Constitution, which Captain White is sworn to defend, do not appear to direct a choice of one course over another.

If Captain White is to analyze his professional responsibility fully, he must also consider whether the boundary condition established by the American value system eliminates one of his possible courses of action. The value of freedom, given the restrictions of military service and the combat situation, provides only general constraints. If the objectives of participation in the conflict are justified by the values of American society, the professional officer has a strong obligation to be loyal and to obey legal orders. In doing so he is defending the value of freedom. The orders in this case are legal under existing criteria.

Another moral value of American society is reflected in the requirement to safeguard the welfare of subordinates. It is the value of individual personality, which attributes intrinsic worth to each person. This value supports a refusal to continue to order soldiers to undertake fatal missions that are also futile. The value of freedom noted in the preceding paragraph suggests that obeying the orders is appropriate. The value of individual personality suggests that it is not. Thus, the values of freedom and individual personality considered together do not appear to point in the same direction.

The most telling moral principle in this situation is perhaps that of individual rights, which derives from the broad values of freedom and individual personality. The principle of individual rights is a formulation of the fundamental moral concept of the Constitution. In considering his own men, Captain White might decide that their rights as human beings preclude the use of his authority to send them into Area B-7. To continue to do so, given Captain White's understanding of the situation, would be to decide that their right to determine their own lives—which they surrendered only to the extent of contributing to the achievement of justified objectives in the conflict—could be justly overridden. Since Captain White believes that the Cemetery missions do not contribute to that goal, and that they are in addition destroying morale and discipline within his unit, the moral argument for refusing to carry out the B-7 patrols appears to outweigh the demand of obedience to orders. The moral requirement in this situation may well result in a truncated military career for Captain White.

Applying the moral values that are implicit in or related to the PME is quite difficult in a case such as this. Acting in accordance with moral conclusions may also be exceedingly difficult. Both, however, are part of the professional obligation inherent in the professional role.

The difficulty of such obligations emerges in a reminiscence reported by Col. Harry Summers. He relates a 1977 conversation between a retired general and Gen. Harold K. Johnson, who was the army's deputy chief of staff for operations during the Vietnam years and later army chief of staff. To the question, "If you had your life to live over again, what would you do differently?" General Johnson responded:

> I remember the day I was ready to go over to the Oval Office and give my four stars to the President and tell him, "You have refused to tell the country they cannot fight a war without mobilization; you have required me to send men into battle with little hope of their ultimate victory; and you have forced us in the military to violate almost every one of the principles of war in Vietnam. Therefore, I resign and will hold a press conference after I walk out of your door."[1]

But, of course, General Johnson did not do so, and, "with a look of anguish," he reportedly said, "I made the typical mistake of believing

I could do more for the country and the Army if I stayed in than if I got out. I am now going to my grave with that burden of lapse of moral courage on my back." Following the morally correct alternative is sometimes more than even exceptional men can accomplish.

One fact is quite clear. The professional role requires that decisions be made and that the moral factors involved in professional decisions be considered as fully as possible. Within the context of the role of the American professional soldier, the choice that is morally correct is also professionally correct.

Case 4: The Ranger

Situation

Captain Black commands a U.S. Army Ranger company. His unit is conducting winter warfare training in the northwest, where a snowstorm has just swept into the training area. The program the company is following includes strenuous mountain climbing under hazardous conditions. During the previous day, two men were seriously injured in training accidents which resulted from the inclement weather and the precipitous mountains where the company is working. Captain Black is considering whether training should be curtailed. The serious injuries to his men have been a grim shock.

One of the combat missions that Captain Black's unit could be assigned involves operations in mountainous terrain. He recognizes that it is essential in terms of combat effectiveness for his unit to learn how to function effectively under extremely adverse conditions. Should they be given a combat mission, they would have to operate in conditions as bad or worse than those they are now experiencing. Further, this is an annual training exercise and thus a once-a-year opportunity to develop critical expertise.

Given the weather conditions, however, further accidents would be almost inevitable. Captain Black is extremely reluctant to order his men into an exercise which will almost certainly result in injuries that could be fatal. Captain Black's higher headquarters, geographically far removed, has given him the authority to make the decision.

Discussion

The obligation to protect the welfare of the individual soldier is a basic principle of the American PME that applies even to rangers. Problems similar to this one are frequently encountered by military commanders and pose troubling questions in some circumstances. In this instance, the obligation to protect the welfare of individual soldiers appears to be in conflict with Captain Black's mission to produce and maintain a capable, experienced combat unit that is prepared as well as possible for its primary function—combat.

As a professional officer and as a commander responsible to superiors, Captain Black has the obligation to produce the best-trained and best-prepared unit possible given his resources. His company has the opportunity to learn how to function in extremely adverse conditions if the training program is continued. Such skills could one day be critical to combat success. The question faced by Captain Black is whether that readiness justifies the risk of training casualties.

Needless to say, the activities of soldiers in armed conflict are exceedingly hazardous, but one could argue that unnecessary exposure to injury and death can hardly be justified in peacetime. On the other hand, the failure to prepare a military unit as thoroughly as possible for the hazards of war also appears inexcusable, both in terms of the professional's responsibility to society and his responsibility to his men.

In this instance, the principle of the welfare of the individual soldier is not necessarily in conflict with the objective of maximizing training effectiveness. The inability of the unit to cope with the rigors of mountainous terrain under adverse weather conditions could eventually be more detrimental to individuals than the current program. From a professional point of view, so long as critical skills are being developed, risks of injury can justifiably be accepted. At some point, damage to unit confidence and morale, in addition to physical risk, will overbalance the tangible training benefits that can be gained from continuing such an exercise. All possible safety precautions in the form of training support should be taken, but a significant degree of risk can be accepted without ethical misgivings. In situations involving critical skills, such risk *should* be accepted.

Case 5: The Base Commander

Situation

Captain Gray commands a naval facility that provides the home port for a number of fleet vessels which rotate from duty in Southeast Asian waters where they support the war effort. In recent months, there has been increasing unrest among the sailors under Captain Gray's command. An underground newsletter which makes its way onto the base has been conducting a virulent campaign against the claimed exploitation of the poor and minorities in America through military service. Captain Gray is aware that a group of black sailors meets regularly and criticizes American participation in the conflict in Southeast Asia. He has been advised by his staff that the rate of disciplinary actions has been increasing over recent weeks, particularly among black sailors. The staff attributes the increase primarily to opposition to American policies concerning Southeast Asia that has been spread by the apparently organized group of black sailors, though such a conclusion is admittedly speculative at this point.

The legal staff of the base has advised Captain Gray that the meetings of the black sailors, though they have not been clandestine or secretive, constitute conspiracy to foster disloyalty and insubordination. The lawyers believe that there is a sufficient basis to institute court martial proceedings. The available evidence makes it quite clear that the black sailors have contended that American participation in the war is morally wrong because the United States is intervening in a civil war in the pursuit of its own interests. They have pointed out that minorities and the poor constitute a much larger percentage of the military services than of the population in general, which they claim is a deliberate policy of the government. The purpose of that policy, they have contended, is to use only the unneeded and unwanted elements of society to fight the country's wars. In addition, the black sailors have encouraged others to bring their complaints and grievances to their group and to allow it to intercede with the chain of command in correcting injustices. The black committee has also requested a meeting with Captain Gray to voice its dissatisfaction and opposition.

In light of recent court decisions, Captain Gray is satisfied that the leaders of the black group have taken actions which may well be held criminal in a court martial. Both the Supreme Court and the Court of Military Appeals have established that the military institution, which is directly responsible for the military security of the United States, cannot permit speech and rhetoric that is detrimental to the accomplishment of assigned missions. Restrictions of First Amendment rights, both censorship and prior restraint, have been upheld. The courts have also upheld suppression of speech in the military if such speech threatens the military subordinate-superior relationship, creates an adverse impact on morale and discipline, or constitutes an immediate danger to national security interests.

Because the black sailors are members of various units, Captain Gray (rather than a subordinate) is considering whether to press charges under the Uniform Code of Military Justice. He is sincerely concerned with the question of fairness. The black sailors apparently have not advocated the overthrow of the government. No existing evidence indicates that they have even urged disobeying orders, though that seems to be implied. Captain Gray has reviewed their files and found that they all seem to perform their duties adequately. Only a few minor disciplinary actions mar their records. By the navy's standards, they are competent sailors.

As a professional, Captain Gray is keenly aware of the moral end served by the American military: the preservation of fundamental rights and liberties. He recognizes that in situations such as this he has an obligation to evaluate the moral as well as the legal status of taking action against sailors, who, in their view, may be exercising what they consider to be the right of free speech.

Discussion

The legal merits of this situation are not the central issue. If the only question were legality, the most reasonable action would be to refer the matter to the court for decision. The primary issue is the resolution of professional obligations. In upholding the Constitution, Captain Gray is necessarily involved with what Chief Justice Earl Warren termed "the vertical reach of the Bill of Rights within the military."[2]

As a professional, Captain Gray is obligated to take the actions he deems necessary in the performance of his immediate duties, as his contribution to the maintenance of national security. If the conduct of his subordinates contributes to the weakening of morale and discipline or directly endangers national security interests, he clearly should counter the effects of such conduct and take action to prevent its continuation. His warrant for action, however, is limited to what is not contrary to the values of American society and the moral principles reflected in the Constitution. The protection of individual rights and liberties (among them the right of free speech) is a protection of such values. Thus, Captain Gray must determine whether the suppression of free speech in this instance is in fact justified. Disagreement with the policies of the government would appear to be a legitimate exercise of free speech, consistent with the equal exercise of such a right by others. Soldiers remain persons in the sense that they are autonomous moral entities capable of rational choice. As such, they retain the right to exercise fundamental freedoms unless it endangers the equal exercise by others.

In a military context, advocacy of mutiny, disobedience, or revolution would usually fall into a class of actions unacceptable under this criterion. Unless such advocacy were a response to sustained institutional or political wrongs, it would be improper and thus the legitimate object of sanctions.

In this case, have the black sailors taken actions that are unacceptable in these terms? They have expressed disagreement with government policies, but they have apparently stopped short of advocating disobedience or mutiny. Disagreement does not constitute disloyalty in the legal sense. There is no clear evidence of an attempt to undermine the chain of command. On the contrary, the black sailors presumably intend to make use of the chain of command to air grievances and complaints. They have requested the opportunity to express their views to the commander, Captain Gray.

Given the limited information presented in this case, the most reasonable course of action for Captain Gray to follow appears to be one in which he grants the request for a meeting with the black sailors. While listening to their views, Captain Gray should present to them his perspective on their actions and make clear the criteria under which their actions will be evaluated. Among those criteria is the actual effect of their meetings and the expression of their views. To the extent that the results constitute a "clear and present danger" to national security interests (ambiguous as such wording is), the conduct of the black sailors will be actionable, both legally and morally.

If, after such a meeting and subsequent counselling by the chain of command, the actions of the black sailors result in the deterioration of morale and discipline or in a threat to specific missions or functions, Captain Gray can and should take action against them as a part of his professional duties.

Several assumptions are made in this discussion. One is that, in Captain Gray's evaluation, American participation in the war in question is not immoral in terms of national values, either in reference to the issues involved in the war or to the conduct of the war itself. Another is that the government is not pursuing unjust and immoral domestic policies. Were either assumption not the case, Captain Gray's position would be more complex to assess. The issues of concern in this case, however, are those of individual rights and command responsibility for combat readiness. In the circumstances described, legal action does not yet appear warranted from a moral point of view.

Case 6: The Technical Expert

Situation

Lieutenant Colonel Brown is a career air force officer who currently works in research and development. His project team is involved in developing and testing a weapons system that is expected to be added to the inventory of the air force. Lieutenant Colonel Brown is responsible for testing the performance of the weapons system in a variety of operational environments.

The development program is a controversial one. The air force sought approval and funding for the weapons system for several years before congressional resistance was overcome. Several key representatives are still adamantly opposed to the continuation of the program and the eventual purchase of the system. The air force, with Pentagon backing, has long insisted that such a weapons system is essential to ensure that it is able to counter certain lethal capabilities which the Soviet bloc has developed and fielded. The weapons system that Lieutenant Colonel Brown is testing is the choice of the air force.

Unfortunately, the weapons system has failed to meet certain minimum requirements established by the Pentagon. When Lieutenant Colonel Brown first reported the difficulties to his project chief, he was told to run the tests again. He was also told that if the weapons system, which had been developed at such cost, were to prove unsatisfactory, the possibility was great that Congress would terminate the entire program in the upcoming budget cycle. In the view of the air force, such a result would critically undermine its future capabilities in relation to the Soviet Union. The project chief went so far as to say that even the president has agreed that the timely procurement of the weapons system is essential to national defense.

While no specific directives have been issued, the project chief has implied that it is his responsibility in this unusual case to ensure that the weapons system meets the minimum requirements. Lieutenant Colonel Brown has identified certain deficiencies that can be corrected over time, but the process will require additional (and costly) development that cannot be accomplished quickly. The project chief has said informally that a flawed but perfectible system would be infinitely preferable to no system at all, but it seems clear that if the system does not meet the minimum requirements, Congress will cut funding entirely in the upcoming budget process. The project chief has temporarily delayed publicaton of the test data, but he can resist pressure for only a limited time.

Lieutenant Colonel Brown also believes that procurement of the weapons system is vitally important. He thinks that it would be an extremely grave error to terminate the program and thus at least to postpone acquisition of the system for the foreseeable future. At the same time, he is instinctively repelled by the thought of doctoring his test results in order to conceal the existing shortcomings of the system.

Discussion

To report the test results in a manner that would betray the purpose of the tests would be a blatant violation of the principle of truth-telling. Arrayed against this clear-cut issue is the more opaque one of determining what action will best serve the purpose of maintaining the security of the nation. While it seems unlikely that any one weapons system would actually be essential to the nation's security, it is certainly possible that someone could believe that to be the case. Lieutenant Colonel Brown may well believe that the congressmen opposed to the weapons system are simply misinformed or are acting from ulterior motives, and that if they clearly understood the situation or acted responsibly, they would have to admit that the program deserved support. He may consider the question of procurement to be one of professional judgment that is not properly decided by laymen. If acquisition of the weapons system is vital to the ability of the military services to perform their defensive function, much might be justified in achieving that goal.

To conceal the actual capabilities of the system as revealed by the tests, however, would be to subvert the principle of subordination to civilian leadership. In effect, Lieutenant Colonel Brown and his project chief would be deciding that they, not the elected representatives of the nation's citizens, should determine how the country should be defended and how it should allocate funds for doing so. From the point of view of the professional ethic and Constitutional authority, it could be strongly argued that even if Lieutenant Colonel Brown and his project chief were correct in their beliefs concerning the need for the weapons system, it would nonetheless be better to report their results accurately and contribute as best they could to an informed debate about what course of action should be followed. Human judgment is indeed fallible, but in a representative democracy, it should be the will of society as interpreted by elected representatives that proves to be in error, not the self-imposed judgments of a few who decide that they know better than all others what "should" be done. If such a view gained currency among those trusted to serve society, democracy would assume a most tenuous existence. Such actions would in the long run certainly undermine rather than "support and defend" the Constitution.

The commitment of the professional officer corps is to support and defend the Constitution. That can hardly be accomplished in any coherent fashion by subverting the consitutional process, however urgent the need may appear to be.

Chapter Nine

Epilogue

Soldiers fight for their fellow soldiers, some of them close friends, some mere acquaintances, but all of them confederates, bonded together by common circumstance. And of course soldiers fight to survive. Seldom do they fight for causes or for abstract values, though they will fight for a strong leader whom they know well. Professional soldiers, however, serve with a concept of commitment to an institution, which is worded variously and roughly, often with some discomfort when the subject comes up in a personal context. Those possessing both commitment and strong character serve in accordance with the professional military ethic. We have many dedicated soldiers in our military services, and they take their professionalism seriously.

It is mainly for them that I have tried to delineate the moral structure that girds and illumines the American professional military ethic. To clarify some of the relationships that determine the guidelines for conduct by members of the American military, I have employed the concept of role-differentiated behavior. My discussion has presented a justification for the military ethic in terms of the value and function of the military institution within American society. As I made clear in chapter 1, I accept Elizabeth Anscombe's position, which claims that the military and the police are essential elements in contemporary human affairs: "For society is essential to human good; and society without coercive power is generally impossible."[1] By applying the concept of role differentiation, I attempted to show that the professional military ethic limits the use of the military's coercive power in important ways.

Analytical devices other than role differentiation could be employed, of course, such as an examination of virtues or an analysis of conduct from the point of view of particular moral theories. Role differentiation provides advantages, however, in that the issue of justification is neatly circumscribed in ways that reflect our thinking about professional conduct. In addition, the perspective I have employed avoids some of the traditional (and unresolved) questions concerning moral truth.

I have concluded that functional requirements necessitate a partially differentiated role for military professionals—one in which professional considerations alter the balance of moral judgments in ways that would be inappropriate for individuals outside the profession. Such differentiation, however, finds justification in the core values of society, which place distinct limits on morally acceptable professional conduct. My study claims, in broad terms, that the American PME is a synthesis of the moral implications generated by the enduring values of American society, the functional requirements of the profession of arms, and the prescriptions of the laws of war.

Some may disagree with the model of ethical relationships I have presented, but I hope that exploring their disagreement clarifies and reinforces their own ethical positions. I remain convinced that the strength of our military leadership and thus our military forces as a whole lies in our commitment to a coherent and stable military ethic.

In the aftermath of Vietnam, the U.S. Army was subjected to painful scrutiny, both from within and from without—for good reason. We had lost a war that we apparently could have won. Among other analyses, that of Richard A. Gabriel and Paul L. Savage found fault with the leadership of the officer corps and traced that shortcoming to an institutional failing: "It has been the failure of the Army as an organization to develop an institutional sense of ethics that is supportive of individual notions of integrity, to ensure that individual officers are trained in a sense of what the ethics of the military institution are."[2]

The army has changed for the better in the decade that has passed since Gabriel and Savage presented their analysis, but the central role of ethics in military professionalism still needs to be stressed. Military professionals should understand clearly the moral framework within which they operate and the military ethic that is to be applied within that framework.

To be morally and logically consistent in applying their professional ethic, members of the military must be able to evaluate problematic situations and develop reasonable conclusions about possible responses. Hard cases arise frequently in military life, as our case studies indicate. We all know that character weaknesses sometimes lead to wrong actions despite a clear grasp of the ethical dimensions of a situation, but recognizing the morally appropriate choice remains the necessary starting point for moral conduct.

In those hard cases involving warfare, the first step in deciding what to do is to recognize what is functionally required to accomplish the mission. The second step is to apply the provisions of the PME, which include the restrictions imposed by the laws of war. To be consistent in resolving troublesome situations, one needs to recognize the role of the laws of war in limiting the acceptable courses of action that are available to fulfill any particular military mission. Members of the American armed forces, by virtue of their commitment to defend the Constitution, are morally and legally obligated to adhere to the laws of war, as we have discussed in considerable detail. The third major step is to recognize the restriction on possible responses imposed by the fundamental values of American society, which I have argued can be described by the terms freedom, equality, individualism, and democracy. These three steps filter out courses of action that are morally inappropriate.

In this nation, the four fundamental social values undergird the military profession and the ethic which guides the activities of its members. Because the armed forces exist to defend and preserve the social realization of those values, the military cannot systematically violate them and succeed in its overall purpose.

Understanding the nature of the professional military ethic and the normative context in which it is applied can make our military leaders more capable and more reliable. Those objectives have motivated my reflection. One question that obviously arises in relation to my discussion (a question that I have not directly addressed) is whether the American military would be well served by the publication of a formal codified ethic. Perhaps the U.S. Army should have several specific codes: one for officers, one for enlisted men, one for combat, one for POWs such as we now have in the Code of Conduct.[3] My own view is that a variety of codes would de-emphasize the importance of each, a result that would not serve well the purposes of the military.

A further question is whether each military service should have its own formal ethical code, or whether one code should apply to all components of the armed forces. Does the air force have special requirements that would dictate a somewhat different code from one appropriate for the navy or one appropriate for the army? Should a broad set of principles apply to all the services, published perhaps by the Department of Defense, with each individual service then promulgating its own supplemental code? Or is it the case either that the level of conduct of the services needs no improvement (a position difficult to maintain) or that a formally codified ethic would not contribute appropriately to attempts at improvement? Such questions have not been ignored in the past, but they need more attention in the future.

Properly applying the professional military ethic, whether formally codified and published or not, will always require judgment, education, training, and experience—the more, the better. Adhering to the ethic under difficult conditions will require both competent leadership and men and women of strong character. Most members of the profession of arms would agree with those two claims, I suspect, and perhaps with one additional conviction as well: without those qualities among its members, neither the military nor the society it defends is likely to succeed. Military leaders will continue to face hard cases in the future. How they handle them will reflect how well those now in uniform have prepared them to make such choices and will play a vital role in determining the overall character and effectiveness of the American military forces in the twenty-first century.

Notes

Chapter 1. Introduction: The Hardest Place

1. Michael Walzer, *Just and Unjust Wars* (New York: Basic Books, 1977), p. xvii.
2. Charles R. Kemble, *The Image of the Army Officer in America* (Westport, Conn.: Greenwood Press, 1973), p. 202.
3. James R. McDonough, *Platoon Leader* (New York: Bantam Books, 1985), p. 139.
4. Omar N. Bradley, *A Soldier's Story* (New York: Henry Holt, 1951), p. 330. Bradley tells the story of Operation COBRA on pp. 330–49.
5. Walzer, *Just and Unjust Wars*, pp. 317–19.
6. Bradley, *A Soldier's Story*, p. 344.
7. Richard Wasserstrom, "Lawyers as Professionals: Some Moral Issues," *Human Rights* 5 (1975): 3.
8. For the clarification provided by this sentence, I am indebted to an unknown reviewer for the University Press of Kansas.
9. As related by C. E. Harris, Jr., in *Applying Moral Theories* (Belmont, Calif.: Wadsworth, 1986), pp. 114–15.
10. Ibid., p. 115.
11. As I will discuss later, aspects of the American PME are expressed and explained in a variety of publications, many of them military manuals and pamphlets, even though there is no formal, comprehensive code for any particular service or the military as a whole. The American PME, then, is a set of moral guidelines for practice that are perpetuated by many informal mechanisms as well as through formal training and schooling within the military system. Anyone wanting to present a comprehensive articulation of the PME would have to draw upon a wide variety of sources.

Chapter 2. The Military as a Profession

1. Alan Goldman, *The Moral Foundations of Professional Ethics* (Totowa, N.J.: Rowman & Littlefield, 1980), p. 18.
2. That military service qualifies as a professional activity is widely accepted. William M. Sullivan implies as much when he says: "The tradi-

tional professions of pre-modern Europe — the church, the law, medicine, and state and military service — were highly honorific because of their perceived centrality to the social and moral order of society. At their best, they were callings to serve the common good" ("Calling or Career: The Tensions of Modern Professional Life," in *Professional Ideals*, ed. Albert Flores [Belmont, Calif.: Wadsworth, 1988], p. 41). Sullivan here also emphasizes the importance of the idea of service to society in the concept of a profession. One reason for examining the concept in some detail in this chapter — despite the largely noncontroversial nature of the claim that the military constitutes a professional group — is that doing so tells us much about the nature of military service.

3. Samuel S. Huntington, *The Soldier and the State* (Cambridge, Mass.: Belknap Press of Harvard University Press, 1957), p. 8. In this book, Huntington states that "the modern officer corps is a professional body and the modern military officer a professional man" (p. 7). He refers to this statement as perhaps the "fundamental thesis" of his book.

4. Samuel S. Huntington, "The Soldier and the State in the 1970's," in *The Changing World of the American Military*, ed. Franklin D. Margiotta (Boulder, Colo.: Westview Press, 1978), p. 16.

5. Huntington, *Soldier and the State*, p. 8.

6. By "norm" I mean a rule or guideline regarding what an individual ought to do under certain conditions; a norm is "an idea that a given behavior is expected because it is right, proper, moral, wise, efficient, technically correct or otherwise defined as desirable" (Frederick L. Bates and Clyde C. Harvey, *The Structure of Social Systems* [New York: Gardner Press, 1975], p. 77). Norms are passive possessions until the agent encounters conditions in which they apply. The conditions may arise from material events in the agent's environment, from social interactions with other agents, or from internal conative or cognitive activity.

7. Roger H. Nye, *The Challenge of Command* (Wayne, N.J.: Avery, 1986), p. 31.

8. Ibid., p. 33.

9. Paul L. Miles, as quoted in Nye, *Challenge of Command*, p. 136.

10. Thomas Pakenham, *The Boer War* (New York: Random House, 1979), pp. xxi–xxii, 521–24. Also see Edgar Holt, *The Boer War* (London: Putnam, 1958), chap. 21.

11. Ruth L. Swaird, *World Military and Social Expenditures* (Washington, D.C.: World Priorities, 1985), p. 11, as cited by Ronald L. Glossup, *Confronting War* (Jefferson, N.C.: McFarland, 1987), p. 312.

12. This view is shared by Glossup, *Confronting War*, p. 4.

13. For a brief but clear discussion of this point, see Lewis S. Sorley, III, "Competence as an Ethical Imperative," *Army* 34 (August 1982): 42–48.

14. Huntington, *Soldier and the State*, p. 16.

15. Bernard Barber, "Some Problems in the Sociology of Professions," in *The Professions in America*, ed. Kenneth S. Lynn (Boston: Houghton Mifflin, 1965), p. 18.

16. The term "professional" most clearly applies to career officers in the combat arms and career officers whose functions are unique to military activity.

17. David K. Hart, "Self-Serving Power and Noblesse Oblige: George C.

Marshall and J. Edgar Hoover" (paper delivered at the Annual Conference, American Society for Public Administration, Portland, Oreg., 19 April 1988).

18. John Adams, "Dissertation on the Canon and the Feudal Law [1765]," in *The Selected Writings of John and John Quincy Adams* (New York: Knopf, 1946), p. 18. Professor David K. Hart brought this quotation to my attention in his unpublished paper, "Self-Serving Power".

19. I am again indebted to David K. Hart, who cites Hanoch Bartow, *Dado: 48 Years and 20 Days*, trans. I. Friedman (Israel: Ma'ariv Book Guild, 1981), p. 34, as the source for this information.

20. Ernest Greenwood, "Attributes of a Profession," in *Man, Work, and Society*, ed. Sigmund Nosow and William H. Form (New York: Basic Books, 1962), pp. 206–7.

21. Flores, *Professional Ideals*, p. 1.

22. This is true even of the lower, perhaps less than fully professional ranks. U.S. Army Training Circular 22-9-1, *Military Professionalism (Platoon and Squad Instruction)* (May 1986), notes that members of the military "are unique in that we are expected to follow higher standards of conduct than civilians are expected to follow" (p. 10). Whether or not this is so, the U.S. Army teaches its members that it is—which is my point at the moment.

23. Greenwood, "Attributes of a Profession," p. 207.

24. Ibid., p. 215.

25. Ibid.

26. Allan R. Millett, *Military Professionalism and Officership in America* (Columbus, Ohio: Mershon Center, 1977), p. 18. For a succinct summary of the historical development of professional armed forces, see Bengt Abrahamsson, *Military Professionalism and Political Power* (Beverly Hills, Calif.: Sage, 1972), pp. 21–23.

27. Ibid., p. 2.

28. Everett C. Hughes, "Professions," in *The Professions in America*, p. 10.

29. Oliver L. North, testimony before the Select Committee of the House and Senate, in *Taking the Stand* (New York: Pocket Books, 1987), pp. 236–45, 251–54, 293–94.

30. Morris Janowitz, *The Professional Soldier: A Social and Political Portrait* (Glencoe, Ill.: Free Press, 1960), p. 6.

Chapter 3.   The Nature of Professional Ethics

1. Let me make clear that by a code of professional ethics I mean just this: the set of rules and standards that govern the conduct of members of a profession. A code may be formal; that is, it may be written down, acknowledged, and published. A code may also be informal and unpublished, yet recognized and adhered to by members of the profession. Informal codes have the character of customs for the group concerned. Needless to say, deeply entrenched customs often have a much more dominating effect on behavior than a formally published code would. In the ensuing discussions, I will try to adhere to the practice of using "professional ethic" to refer to the actual set of rules and standards governing conduct within a profession, whether they have been written down in a formal document or not, and I will use "formal code" or name a particular published document when I refer to a for-

mally propagated written code. The professional military ethic (PME) is the implicit or explicit set of rules and standards accepted by military professionals, taught to entering soldiers with varying degrees of complexity based upon rank and experience, and generally held up as the model for professional conduct. The American PME has not been formally codified, but it plays a dominant role in professional activity.

2. Ernest Greenwood, "Attributes of a Profession," in *Man, Work, and Society*, ed. Sigmund Nosow and William H. Form (New York: Basic Books, 1962), p. 6.

3. See American Institute of Certified Public Accountants, *Professional Standards*, vol. 2 (Chicago: Commerce Clearing House, 1977) and AICPA, *Rules of Conduct, Bylaws* (New York: AICPA, Inc., 1978). See also the engineers' code reprinted and discussed in *Ethical Problems in Engineering*, ed. Robert Baum and Albert Flores (Troy, N.Y.: Center for the Study of Human Dimensions of Science and Technology, Rennselaer Polytechnic Institute, 1978).

4. American Medical Association, *Principles of Medical Ethics of the A.M.A.* (Chicago: American Medical Association, 1970).

5. The concepts in (1) and (2) are discussed by Bengt Abrahamsson, *Military Professionalism and Political Power* (Beverly Hills, Calif.: Sage, 1972), p. 69.

6. From *The Trial of Queen Caroline*, vol. 2, ed. J. Nightingale (London: Albion Press, 1821), p. 8, as quoted by Charles Fried, *Right and Wrong* (Cambridge, Mass.: Harvard University Press, 1978), p. 177.

7. Sam C. Sarkesian, *The Professional Army Officer in a Changing Society* (Chicago: Nelson-Hall, 1975), pp. 240–41.

8. Sam C. Sarkesian, "An Empirical Reassessment of Military Professionalism," in *The Changing World of the American Military*, ed. Franklin D. Margiotta (Boulder, Colo.: Westview Press, 1978), p. 43.

9. Samuel S. Huntington, *The Soldier and the State* (Cambridge, Mass.: Belknap Press of Harvard University Press, 1957), p. 73.

10. See Edward Sherman, "Free Speech and the Military," *Update* 5 (Winter 1981): 25–27, 33–34.

11. U.S. Army War College, *Study on Military Professionalism* (Carlisle Barracks, Pa.: U.S. Army War College, 1970), pp. 30–31.

12. Huntington, *Soldier and the State*, p. 61.

13. Ibid., p. 60.

14. For further discussion of the "military mind," see Maury Feld, "Professionalism, Nationalism and the Alienation of the Military," in *Armed Forces and Society*, ed. Jacques van Doorn (The Hague: Mouton, 1968), pp. 55–70; Morris Janowitz and Roger W. Littel, *Sociology and the Military Establishment*, rev. ed. (New York: Russell Sage Foundation, 1965), pp. 20–27, 31–76; Jacques van Doorn, "Ideology and the Military," in *On Military Ideology*, ed. Morris Janowitz and Jacques van Doorn (Rotterdam, The Netherlands: Rotterdam University Press, 1971), pp. xv–xxix.

15. Abrahamsson, *Military Professionalism*, pp. 64–65.

16. Huntington, *Soldier and the State*, p. 65.

17. Ibid., p. 68.

18. Abrahamsson, *Military Professionalism*, p. 111.

19. Ibid., pp. 76–79 in particular.

20. "Effective" is a relative term, needless to say. The expression refers to an ideal level of effectiveness, since history is replete with examples of armed forces seriously deficient in such characteristics that were nonetheless victorious in a given battle or conflict.

Chapter 4. The American Professional Military Ethic

1. Several studies reveal that to be the case. These include the following: U.S. Army War College, *Study on Military Professionalism* (Carlisle Barracks, Pa.: U.S. Army War College, 1970); John N. Moellering, "Future Civil-Military Relations: The Army Turns Inward?" *Military Review* 53 (July 1973): 68–83; Bruce M. Russett, "Political Perspectives of US Military and Business Elites," *Armed Forces and Society* 1 (Fall 1974): 79–108; and Franklin D. Margiotta, "A Military Elite in Transition: Air Force Leaders in the 1970's," *Armed Forces and Society* 2 (Winter 1976): 155–184.

2. The concept of interpreting the Constitution for application to changing social, political, and economic circumstances is strongly criticized by some legal scholars. Strict constructionists have long argued that an interpretive view of the Constitution is fundamentally in error, that the creation of new standards and new law without a clear textual reference in the Constitution violates the very concept of constitutionality. In their view, the Constitution is a specific, unchanging document that is to be applied as written. If one accepts their view, my contention that there are certain fundamental, unchanging principles reflected in the Constitution gains even more support.

3. Leonard W. Levy, *Judgments: Essays on American Constitutional History* (Chicago: Quadrangle Books, 1972), p. 71.

4. Jethro K. Lieberman, *Understanding Our Constitution* (New York: Walker, 1967), p. 14. Fundamentally, I contend that this is true for the principles identified in this discussion. It would be both naive and erroneous, however, not to recognize that a broadly stated principle can be admirable or destructive in application. How we characterize it will be a function of circumstances. Thus, "Never give up" in some situations may be considered an injunction that appeals to the tenacious, courageous, essentially noble fire of the human spirit. The battle of Stalingrad, however, was an inhumane example of the capacity of human nature to produce suffering and barbarism. For a caustic view of the fate of the Bill of Rights in judicial application, see William O. Douglas, "The Bill of Rights Is Not Enough," in *The Great Rights*, ed. Edmund Cahn (New York: Macmillan, 1963). Nonetheless, in considering the ideal standards of the PME, certain broad moral principles which have not changed do seem to be identifiable in the Constitution.

5. James L. Elston, "The Warren Court and Civil Rights: Era of Positive Constitutionalism and Egalitarianism," *Journal of Thought* 8 (Summer 1977): 30.

6. Though, admittedly, the extension of the concept of who is included among the holders of equal rights has indeed changed. One need only remember that many of the primary authors of the Declaration of Independence were slave owners to realize that racial discrimination has always belied the rhetoric which proclaimed that all human beings possess natural rights. In

this sense, the Civil War era and the mid-twentieth century can be seen as periods of dramatic change in the concept of equality. I would argue, however, that the moral principle of equality itself did not change; rather, the extension of the principle in social application changed. More critically, American society has slowly and unevenly moved toward the full instantiation of such principles in practice in its social institutions.

7. For a brief but illuminating discussion of the protection afforded individual rights by the Constitution, see Zechariah Chaffee, Jr., *How Human Rights Got into the Constitution* (Boston: Boston University Press, 1952).

8. Sotiros A. Barber, *On What the Constitution Means* (Baltimore: Johns Hopkins Press, 1984), p. 127.

9. Clinton Rossiter, *Seedtime of the Republic* (New York: Harcourt, Brace, 1953), p. 375.

10. David A. J. Richards, "Reverse Discrimination and Compensatory Justice: Constitutional and Moral Theory," in *The Value of Justice*, ed. Charles A. Kelbley (New York: Fordham University Press, 1979), pp. 104–5. For a scholarly discussion of this issue, see Levy, *Judgments: Essays on American Constitutional History*, particularly "The Fourteenth Amendment and the Bill of Rights" and the essays of Part II and Part III.

11. Arthur E. Sutherland, *Constitutionalism in America* (New York: Blaisdell, 1965), p. 469.

12. I intend here a broad sense of the "rule of law" concept. The fundamental issue is that of the priority of law, to which all governmental agencies and positions are subordinate—including in particular the most powerful, such as the military services and the office of the president. In referring to the power of the Court in this context, I do not mean to invoke the controversial issue of judicial review.

13. Richards, "Reverse Discrimination," pp. 105–6.

14. Ibid., p. 107.

15. Ibid.

16. Ibid.

17. For a specific declaration of the rights held under the doctrine of natural rights during this period in America, see the Virginia Declaration of Rights, 1776, which can be found, among other places, in F. N. Thorpe, *Federal and State Constitutions, Colonial Charters, and Other Organic Laws*, vol. 7 (Washington, D.C.: GPO, 1909), pp. 3812–3814.

18. U.S. Army War College, *Study on Military Professionalism*, pp. 28–29.

19. Department of Defense, *The Armed Forces Officer*, DoD GEN-36 (Washington, D.C.: GPO, 1975), p. 3.

20. Charles R. Kemble, *The Image of the Army Officer in America* (Westport, Conn.: Greenwood Press, 1973), pp. 24–25.

21. Sir John Winthrop Hackett, *The Profession of Arms* (London: Times Publishing, 1962), p. 38.

22. U.S. Army War College, *Study on Military Professionalism*, p. iii. The authors of the War College study found it difficult to articulate the implications of this motto. An unusually perceptive examination is presented by James R. Golden, "The Future Demands of Military Professionalism: The Views of an Army Major," in *The Changing World of the American Military*, ed. Franklin D. Margiotta (Boulder, Colo.: Westview Press, 1978), pp. 395–412.

23. Sam C. Sarkesian, "An Empirical Reassessment of Military Professionalism," in *Changing World of the American Military*, p. 48.

24. Golden, "Future Demands," p. 398.

25. Melville A. Drisko, Jr., *An Analysis of Professional Military Ethics: Their Importance, Development, and Inculcation* (Carlisle Barracks, Pa.: U.S. Army War College, 1977), p. 4.

26. Golden, "Future Demands," pp. 404–5.

27. Ibid., p. 409.

28. Lewis S. Sorley, III, "Competence as Ethical Imperative: Issues of Professionalism," in *Military Ethics and Professionalism: A Collection of Essays*, ed. James Brown and Michael J. Collins (Washington, D.C.: National Defense University Press, 1981), p. 39.

29. Morris Janowitz, *The Professional Soldier: A Social and Political Portrait* (Glencoe, Ill.: Free Press, 1960), p. 233.

30. See Charles H. Coates and Roland J. Pellegrin, *Military Sociology* (University Park, Md.: Social Science Press, 1965); Samuel S. Huntington, *The Soldier and the State* (Cambridge, Mass.: Belknap Press of Harvard University Press, 1957); Sam C. Sarkesian, *The Military-Industrial Complex: A Reassessment* (Beverly Hills, Calif.: Sage, 1972); John M. Swomley, Jr., *The Military Establishment* (Boston: Beacon Press, 1964); Adam Yarmolinsky, *The Military Establishment* (New York: Harper & Row, 1971), pp. 8–15, chap. 5, and especially chap. 16.

31. Within the UCMJ, however, there is a well-known provision, Article 133, which provides for punishment of "conduct unbecoming to an officer and a gentleman." While this provision is as vague in statement as any punitive article is likely to be, the courts have long held its validity, primarily because they have recognized that there is a distinct, traditional military ethic that is established and accepted for military officers. Thus, while the UCMJ is not part of the PME, it certainly recognizes the binding quality of the American PME and the existence of a separate set of standards.

32. Neither the air force nor the navy attempt to capture the elements of the professional ethic in service-wide publications to the extent that the army does, and as we can see, the army provides only general guidance. Education concerning professional ethics and military values in the navy and air force appears to take place primarily in the professional school system, where individual faculty members and offices generate course materials that examine issues in professional ethics. Such materials are not, however, published service-wide, and they change frequently as faculty members are replaced through rotation.

Chapter 5.   The Moral Character of the Laws of War

1. In an opinion that has not been questioned by civilized nations and has been supported in the actions of the United Nations, the International Military Tribunal at Nuremberg following World War II declared that "the conventions of Hague and Geneva were merely declaratory of pre-existing and well-established laws 'recognized by all civilized nations,' and that the laws of war are binding on all, irrespective of whether a particular government has signed a particular convention" (Marjorie M. Whiteman, *Digest of*

International Law, vol. 11, Department of State Publication 8367 [Washington, D.C.: GPO, 1968], p. 886).

2. Under Article VI, Clause 2 of the U.S. Constitution, treaties relating to the laws of war to which the United States is a signatory have a force equal to that of laws passed by Congress. As early as 1900, the U.S. Supreme Court ruled in *The Paquette Habana,* 175 U.S. 677, that international law is in fact the law of the United States.

3. Carl von Clausewitz, *On War,* ed. Anatol Rapoport (Baltimore: Penguin Books, 1968], p. 101.

4. Whiteman, *Digest of International Law,* vol. 10, p. 288.

5. U.S. Army, *The Law of Land Warfare,* FM 27-10 (Washington, D.C.: 1956], p. 7.

6. Leon Friedman, ed., *The Law of War: A Documentary History,* vol. 1 (New York: Random House, 1972], p. 3.

7. Sidney Bailey, *Prohibitions and Restraints in War* (Oxford: Oxford University Press, 1972], pp. 4–7.

8. Ibid., p. 9.

9. For a detailed, careful examination of the concept of pacifism, see Jenny Teichman, *Pacifism and the Just War: A Study in Applied Philosophy* (Oxford: Basil Blackwell, 1986].

10. The history of the development of just-war theory is presented clearly in James Turner Johnson, *Just War Tradition and the Restraint of War: A Moral and Historical Inquiry* (Princeton, N.J.: Princeton University Press, 1981].

11. A. Pearce Higgins, *The Hague Peace Conferences and Other International Conferences Concerning the Laws and Usages of War: Texts of Conventions with Commentaries* (Cambridge, Mass.: Cambridge University Press, 1909], p. 256.

12. Telford Taylor, "Foreword," in *The Law of War: A Documentary History,* p. 6.

13. Richard I. Miller, *The Law of War* (Lexington, Mass.: D.C. Heath, 1975], p. 6.

14. Morris Greenspan, *The Modern Law of Land Warfare* (Berkeley: University of California Press, 1959], p. 11.

15. Geneva Convention for the Amelioration of the Condition of the Wounded and Sick in Armed Forces in the Field, 12 August 1949, Article 149; Geneva Convention for the Amelioration of the Conditions of Wounded, Sick, and Shipwrecked Members of Forces at Sea, 12 August 1949, Article 50; Geneva Convention Relative to the Treatment of Prisoners of War, 12 August 1949, Article 129; Geneva Convention Relative to the Protection of Civilian Persons in Time of War, 12 August 1949, Article 146.

16. A further form of sanction has been developing since World War II. The European Court of Human Rights, while not specifically concerned with war crimes, is a forum in which abuses of civilized behavior in armed conflict can be identified and dealt with in the international forum. An Inter-American Court of Human Rights, a special organ of the Organization of American States, entered into force in 1978. Such regional courts of an international nature may develop as an effective source of sanctions in addition to the cooperative actions possible through actions by the United Nations. See Carlos Alberto Dunshee de Abranches, "The Inter-American Court of

Human Rights," and Thomas Burgenthal, "The American and European Conventions on Human Rights: Similarities and Differences," *American University Law Review* 30 (Fall 1980).

17. Bert A. Röling, "Aspects of Criminal Responsibility for Violations of the Laws of War," in *The New Humanitarian Law of Armed Conflict*, ed. Antonio Cassese (Napoli, Italy: Editoriale Scientifica, 1979), p. 227n.

18. Bailey, *Prohibitions and Restraints*, p. 62.

19. Greenspan, *Modern Law of Land Warfare*, p. 4.

20. As quoted by Bailey, in *Prohibitions and Restraints*, p. 65.

21. As quoted by Greenspan, in *Modern Law of Land Warfare*, p. 6.

22. Greenspan, *Modern Law of Land Warfare*, pp. 7–8.

23. Ibid., as quoted, p. 8.

24. U.S. Air Force, *International Law—The Conduct of Armed Conflict and Air Operations*, AF Pamphlet 110-31 (Washington, D.C.: 1976), p. 11-1. Nations have adopted the practice of formally acceding to international treaties with reservations—that is, with stipulations about their understanding of possibly ambiguous wording or with qualifications about their acceptance of specific provisions of treaties otherwise accepted as binding.

25. As of December 1986, of the 171 nations in the international community, 22 had ratified Protocol I and 44 more had acceded to it; 20 states had ratified Protocol II and 40 had acceded to it. Neither the U.S. nor the USSR have ratified either, though both were signatories. In 1987, President Reagan called on the U.S. Senate to ratify Protocol II.

26. Article I, Hague Convention III, 1907.

27. The British, West German, and U.S. military manuals that address the laws of war all declare that nuclear weapons as such are not prohibited in the existing laws of war. Their use nonetheless would be governed by the general laws of war, a fact which none dispute. The uses of nuclear weapons planned by the nuclear powers would involve noncombatants in ways that would appear to violate the laws. While Protocol I to the Geneva Conventions of 12 August 1949 has not changed from the status of "being considered" to being ratified by the states of international society, the movement is steady. Including declarations, seventy-three states have formally accepted the protocol, Part IV of which essentially prohibits all attacks on the civilian population and threats of violence intended to terrorize civilians. So long as the use of nuclear weapons remains indiscriminate, the provisions of Protocol I would appear to prohibit their employment—and perhaps even the threat of their employment. For a detailed discussion, see Tony Carty, "Legality and Nuclear Weapons: Doctrines of Nuclear War Fighting," in *Ethics and Defence*, ed. Howard Davis (Oxford: Basil Blackwell, 1986).

28. In any consistent application of the laws of war, the use of nuclear weapons would appear to be a violation, though I will not argue the point here.

29. Relatively few nations have as yet ratified the protocols. The United States, though a signatory to the protocols in 1977, has not yet formally ratified the documents and filed the ratification in Geneva.

30. Friedman, *The Law of War*, vol. 1, p. 161.

31. Immanuel Kant, "Perpetual Peace," in *Kant's Political Writings*, ed. Hans Reiss, trans. H. B. Nisbet (Cambridge: Cambridge University Press, 1977), p. 32.

32. U.S. Army, *Law of Land Warfare*, p. 22.

33. Ibid., p. 23.

34. Ibid., p. 22.

35. Ibid.

36. Friedman, *The Law of War*, vol. 1, p. 595.

37. So called in recognition of the Russian jurist F. F. Martens, president of the 1899 Hague Conventions.

38. Friedman, *The Law of War*, vol. 1, p. 309.

39. U.S. Air Force, *International Law*, pp. 1–6.

40. Ibid.

41. Ibid., p. 11-4.

42. Greenspan, *Modern Law of Land Warfare*, p. 22.

43. This point is presented forcefully in the Preamble to Hague Convention No. IV (1907).

44. Military necessity is not a fourth type to be added to Leibniz's three categories: logical, physical, and moral. If the action required by military necessity is not accomplished, no logical, physical, or moral law is violated. In any technical sense, the term "military necessity" is a misnomer, for it concerns neither a necessary proposition nor a state of affairs that cannot be other than it is. The notion implicit in this term is that of a necessary condition.

One can identify two broad contexts in which the term "necessity" is used in connection with warfare — that of military necessity and that of the necessity of state self-preservation. The sense of necessity is not the same in both. Military necessity connotes indispensability. If, on the conditional proposition, "if A, then B," A is defined as a state of affairs in which the war is won, or the objective is achieved, or the enemy is defeated, then B is an act or state of affairs that constitutes a necessary condition for the realization of A. Needless to say, that B is a necessary condition is, in practice, a matter of more or less reliable judgment. At best, it is a conclusion based on a process of induction involving a very narrow and incomplete database.

The sense of the term in the "necessity" of state self-preservation carries the idea of conditionality also, but it adds a very important notion that changes its meaning: the notion of inevitability. When necessity is used in this context, a law *is* claimed to have been violated if the action required is not taken. The laws involved in such cases are moral laws or rules. Just as individuals are sometimes held to have not only a right but also an obligation to preserve themselves (consider John Locke, *Two Treatises of Government*, Book II, Chapter I), states as corporate entities are held to have an absolute moral obligation to act in self-preservation, or to be so constituted that they can act in no other way when their existence is threatened. When necessity is used in this sense, the clear implication is that no other action is possible, from either a moral or literal point of view — hence the notion of inevitability. This sense is quite different from the hypothetical one that is appropriate with respect to the term "military necessity." The indiscriminate use of the term "necessity" sometimes confuses discussions of the laws of war.

45. HP2, applied directly to actions, functions just as the Happiness Principle (or Pleasure Principle) does in act utilitarian theory. Minimizing suffering is merely the converse of maximizing happiness, so that if HP2

were the sole basis for deciding what to do in situations involving moral choice in warfare, we would be concerned with a particular application of utilitarianism. Our discussion has shown that this is not the case. Further, if HP2 were the principle from which all the laws of war were derived, we would be concerned with a form of rule utilitarianism, with the laws of war being the rules which, all things being considered, best served HP2 (that is, such a situation would be the ideal, though it certainly has not been achieved in practice). On the contrary, HP1 appears to have priority over HP2 when the two principles conflict. While we have not examined all such instances (nor would that be possible), the representative cases presented make that a reasonable conclusion. The point argued here is that analysis of the current laws of war reveals that HP1 has priority over HP2 in the formulation of such laws.

46. Richard B. Brandt, "Utilitarianism and the Rules of War," *Philosophy and Public Affairs* 1 (Winter 1972): 145–65.

47. Adopting a rule to be followed without exception could be the result of rule utilitarian reasoning, which is probably the position Brandt would take concerning HP1.

48. U.S. Air Force, *International Law*, pp. 1–10.

49. Dietrich Schindler, ed., *The Laws of Armed Conflict* (Geneva: Henry Dunant Institute, 1973), p. 133.

50. U.S. Army, *Law of Land Warfare*, p. 20.

51. Ibid., p. 19.

52. Schindler, *Laws of Armed Conflict*, p. 142.

53. Ibid.

54. Hague Regulations Respecting the Laws and Customs of War on Land, Annex to Hague Convention IV, 18 October 1907, Article 26.

55. U.S. Army, *Law of Land Warfare*, p. 20.

56. Under Protocol I of the Protocols to the Geneva Conventions of 1949, the bombing mission would appear even more clearly illegal. Article 51(4) prohibits "indiscriminate attacks," which are those employing a method which cannot be directed at a specific military objective. The B-52 strike appears, in these circumstances, to be such an attack. Article 51(5) goes further, declaring an "indiscriminate attack" to be one which treats as a single military objective a number of clearly separate and distinct military objectives located in the same area.

Chapter 6.   The Values of American Society

1. William C. Mitchell, *The American Polity* (New York: Free Press of Glencoe, 1962), p. 105.

2. David Hume, *Essays Moral, Political, and Literary*, ed. T. H. Green and T. H. Grose, vol. 1 (London: Longmans, 1882), p. 248.

3. Mitchell, *The American Polity*, p. 376.

4. Robin M. Williams, Jr., "Values and Modern Education in the United States," in *Values in America*, ed. Donald Barrett (Notre Dame, Ind.: University of Notre Dame Press, 1961), p. 63.

5. Seymour M. Lipset, *The First New Nation* (New York: Basic Books, 1963), p. 123.

6. Robin Williams, for example, in *American Society: A Sociological Perspective* (New York: Alfred A. Knopf, 1958), says that values are "modes of organizing conduct—meaningful, affectively invested pattern principles that guide human action" (p. 375).

7. Gerald E. Critoph, "The Contending Americas," in *Values in America*, p. 18.

8. Ralph Barton Perry, *Realms of Value* (New York: Greenwood Press, 1968 reprint), p. 273.

9. Ibid., p. 285.

10. Ibid., p. 286.

11. Williams, *American Society*, pp. 436–37.

12. Ibid., p. 419.

13. Lipset, *The First New Nation*, p. 101.

14. Perry, *Realms of Value*, p. 286.

15. Williams, *American Society*, p. 415.

16. John Locke, *Two Treatises of Government*, ed. Peter Laslett (New York: New American Library, 1960), pp. 374–75. For an extended discussion of the pervasive influence of individualism, see Elizabeth Wolgast, *The Grammar of Justice* (Ithaca, N.Y.: Cornell University Press, 1987), chap. 1.

17. Williams, *American Society*, p. 433.

18. Perry, *Realms of Value*, p. 273.

19. Eugene Kamka, ed., *Nationalism* (Canberra: Australian National University Press, 1973), p. 15.

20. Williams, *American Society*, p. 429.

21. This particular trait has been commented upon extensively by many people, including Alexis de Tocqueville, James Bryce, Harold Laski, Gunnar Myrdal, and Margaret Mead.

22. Williams, *American Society*, p. 399f.

23. See Milton Rokeach, "Values in American Society," part 2, in *The Nature of Human Values* (New York: Free Press, 1973), and Norman Feather, *Values in Education and Society* (New York: Free Press, 1975).

24. U.S. Air Force, *International Law—The Conduct of Armed Conflict and Air Operations*, AF Pamphlet 110-31 (Washington, D.C., 19 November 1976), p. 11–4.

Chapter 7.   Justifying Military Decisions

1. Maxwell D. Taylor, "A Do-It-Yourself Professional Code for the Military," *Parameters* 10 (December 1980): 11.

2. Ibid.

3. Ibid., p. 13.

4. Ibid., p. 14.

5. Alan Goldman, *The Moral Foundations of Professional Ethics* (Totowa, N.J.: Rowman & Littlefield, 1980), p. 24.

6. See D. Clayton James, *The Years of MacArthur* (Boston: Houghton Mifflin, 1970); William Manchester, *American Caesar* (Boston: Little, Brown, 1978); or Trumbull Higgins, *Korea and the Fall of MacArthur* (New York: Oxford University Press, 1960).

7. Marjorie M. Whiteman, *Digest of International Law*, vol. 10, Department of State Publication 8367 (Washington, D.C.: GPO, 1968), p. 308.

8. Goldman, *Moral Foundations*, p. 49.

9. Ibid., p. 57.

10. Ibid.

11. Civilians, as noncombatants who possess certain rights *because* they are noncombatants, may not participate in combat operations during wartime unless they are directly defending their homes and their state against invasion. If they take up arms "spontaneously" for that purpose, they are entitled to POW status if captured and cannot be tried for crimes against the invading force, as a civilian could otherwise be tried if he or she bore arms and used them against a military force without being a member of an organized military unit.

12. Goldman, *Moral Foundations*, p. 90.

13. Ibid., p. 117.

14. Ibid., pp. 112–37.

15. Ibid., p. 120.

16. Ibid., p. 122.

17. The literal translation is as follows: "Reasons of war go before the manners of war." The doctrine maintains that the needs of war take precedence over the laws and customs of warfare.

18. James L. Narel, "Values and the Professional Soldier," *Parameters* 11 (December 1981): 76.

19. I contend that that is so, and that any comprehensive examination of the American PME reveals that it is so, despite the functional explanation provided in the primary U.S. Army document concerning the subject, FM 100-1, *The Army* (August 1986). The discussion there captures just one aspect of the duty principle under the PME, that of accomplishing assignments as effectively as possible. In doing so, the passage is somewhat misleading. "Duty is obedience and disciplined performance, despite difficulty or danger. It is doing what should be done when it should be done. Duty is a personal act of responsibility manifested by accomplishing all assigned tasks to the fullest of one's capability, meeting all commitments, and exploiting opportunities to improve oneself for the good of the group. Duty requires each of us to accept responsibility not only for our own actions, but also for the actions of those entrusted to our care" (p. 22).

20. Military necessity refers to the rationale justifying actions that must be taken if military objectives are to be achieved with minimum loss of time, life, and resources. Proportionality refers to the moral limitation on action that requires that the injury and cost incurred by the means employed to achieve an objective be proportional to the importance of that objective.

21. Even strong defenders of rights sometimes compromise in this regard. For a case in point, see Michael Walzer, *Just and Unjust Wars* (New York: Basic Books, 1977). Walzer argues throughout most of his book that guidance for conduct should adhere to the claim that "life and liberty are something like absolute values" (p. xvi). But when national survival is at stake, he accepts the concept of "supreme emergency" under which agents of the state may justifiably do whatever is necessary to avoid defeat (see chapter 16).

22. William Frankena, *Ethics* (Englewood Cliffs, N.J.: Prentice-Hall, 1963), p. 98.

23. This argument does not deny that in some situations, certain rights *override* others. In our society, the principle of taxation, the exercise of eminent domain, and the policy of military conscription are but a few of many examples. But numbers alone are not the explanation for such cases.

24. The principle of greatest equal liberty, long a staple of the classical liberal position and now the libertarian view, states that all persons have a right to the greatest liberty in their actions consistent with equal liberty for all others.

Chapter 8.   The Rubber and the Road: Case Studies

1. Harry G. Summers, Jr., "Palmer, Karnow, and Herrington: A Review of Recent Vietnam War Histories," *Parameters* 15 (Spring 1985): 81.

2. Earl Warren, "The Bill of Rights and the Military," in *The Great Rights*, ed. Edmund Cahn (New York: Macmillan, 1963), p. 95.

Chapter 9.   Epilogue

1. Elizabeth Anscombe, "War and Murder," in *War, Morality, and the Military Profession*, 2d ed., ed. Malham Wakin (Boulder, Colo.: Westview Press, 1986), p. 288.

2. Richard A. Gabriel and Paul L. Savage, *Crisis in Command: Management in the Army* (New York: Hill & Wang, 1978), p. 104.

3. Nicholas Fotion and Gerard Elfstrom, in *Military Ethics: Guidelines for Peace and War* (Boston: Routledge & Kegan Paul, 1986), chap. 3, suggest that the military needs several different formal, short, easily comprehended sets of rules for its members that would apply in appropriate contexts.

Bibliography

American Bar Association. *Code of Professional Responsibility*. Chicago: American Bar Association, 1969.

American Medical Association. *Principles of Medical Ethics of the A.M.A.* Chicago: American Medical Association, 1970.

Bailey, Sidney. *Prohibitions and Restraints in War*. Oxford: Oxford University Press, 1972.

Barber, Bernard. "Some Problems in the Sociology of the Professions." In *The Professions in America*, edited by Kenneth S. Lynn. Boston: Houghton Mifflin, 1965.

Barrett, Donald, ed. *Values in America*. Notre Dame, Ind.: University of Notre Dame Press, 1961.

Bentham, Jeremy. "An Introduction to the Principles of Morals and Legislation." In *British Moralists, 1650–1800*, edited by D. D. Raphael. Oxford: Clarendon Press, 1969.

Bledstein, Burton J. *The Culture of Professionalism*. New York: W. W. Norton, 1976.

Bradley, Omar N. *A Soldier's Story*. New York: Henry Holt, 1951.

Brandt, Richard B. "Utilitarianism and the Rules of War." *Philosophy and Public Affairs* 1 (Winter 1972): 145–65.

Braun, William N. *An Ethical Army Leadership—Real or Wanting?* Individual Study Project. Carlisle Barracks, Pa.: U.S. Army War College, 1988.

Brierly, J. L. *The Law of Nations*. 6th ed. New York: Oxford University Press, 1963.

Brown, James, and Michael J. Collins, eds. *Military Ethics and Professionalism: A Collection of Essays*. Washington, D.C.: National Defense University Press, 1981.

Cassese, Antonio, ed. *The New Humanitarian Law of Armed Conflict*. Napoli, Italy: Editoriale Scientifica, 1979.

Clausewitz, Carl von. *On War*. Edited by Anatol Rapoport. Baltimore: Penguin Books, 1968.

Coates, Charles H., and Roland J. Pellegrin. *Military Sociology*. University Park, Md.: Social Science Press, 1965.

Cramer, Walter E. *The Year of Values*. Individual Study Project. Carlisle Barracks, Pa.: U.S. Army War College, 1986.

Crocker, Lawrence. *The Army Officer's Guide*. Harrisburg, Pa.: Stackpole Books, 1979.

Downey, Robert S. *Roles and Values*. London: Methuen, 1971.

Downey, William G., Jr. "The Law of War and Military Necessity." *American Journal of International Law* 47 (1953): 251–62.

Drisko, Melville A., Jr. *An Analysis of Professional Military Ethics: Their Importance, Development, and Inculcation*. Carlisle Barracks, Pa.: U.S. Army War College, 1977.

Dunbar, N. C. H. "The Significance of Military Necessity in the Law of War." *Judicial Review* 67 (1955): 201–12.

Dworkin, Ronald. *Taking Rights Seriously*. Cambridge, Mass.: Harvard University Press, 1977.

Dyck, Arthur J. "Ethical Bases of the Military Profession." *Parameters* 10 (March 1980): 39–46.

Elston, James L. "The Warren Court and Civil Rights: Era of Positive Constitutionalism and Egalitarianism." *Journal of Thought* 8 (Summer 1977): 19–39.

Falk, Richard A. *Law, Morality, and War in the Contemporary World*. New York: Frederick A. Praeger, 1963.

———. "The Shimoda Case: A Legal Appraisal of the Atomic Attacks on Hiroshima and Nagasaki." In *International Law in the Twentieth Century*, edited by Leo Gross. New York: Appleton-Century-Crofts, 1969.

Feather, Norman. *Values in Education and Society*. New York: Free Press, 1975.

Feld, Maury. *The Structure of Violence: Armed Forces as Social Systems*. Beverly Hills, Calif. Sage, 1977.

Feld, Maury. "Professionalism, Nationalism, and the Alienation of the Military." In *Armed Forces and Society*, edited by Jacques van Doorn. The Hague: Mouton, 1968.

Fotion, Nicholas, and Gerard Elfstrom. *Military Ethics: Guidelines for Peace and War*. Boston: Routledge & Kegan Paul, 1986.

Frankena, William. *Ethics*. Englewood Cliffs, N.J.: Prentice Hall, 1963.

Fried, Charles. *Right and Wrong*. Cambridge, Mass.: Harvard University Press, 1978.

Friedman, Leon, ed. *The Law of War: A Documentary History*. 2 vols. New York: Random House, 1972.

Gabriel, Richard A. *To Serve with Honor*. Westport, Conn.: Greenwood Press, 1982.

Gerke, Teitler. *The Genesis of the Professional Officer's Corps*. Beverly Hills, Calif.: Sage, 1977.

Goldman, Alan. *The Moral Foundations of Professional Ethics*. Totowa, N.J.: Rowman & Littlefield, 1980.

Greenspan, Morris. *The Modern Law of Land Warfare*. Berkeley: University of California Press, 1959.

Greenwood, Ernest. "Attributes of a Profession." In *Man, Work, and Society*, edited by Sigmund Nosow and William H. Form. New York: Basic Books, 1962.

Hackett, Sir John Winthrop. *The Profession of Arms*. London: Times Publishing, 1962.

Handy, Rollo. *Value Theory and the Behavioral Sciences*. Springfield, Ill.: Charles C. Thomas, 1969.

Harris, C. E., Jr. *Applying Moral Theories*. Belmont, Calif.: Wadsworth, 1986.

Hartjen, Raymond C., Jr. *Ethics in Organizational Leadership*. Individual Study Project. Carlisle Barracks, Pa.: U.S. Army War College, 1984.

Hartle, Anthony E. "A Military Ethic in an Age of Terror". *Parameters* 17 (Summer 1987): 68–76.

———. "Humanitarianism and the Laws of War." *Philosophy* 235 (1986): 109–16.

Higgins, A. Pearce. *The Hague Peace Conferences and Other International Conferences Concerning the Laws and Usages of War: Texts of Conventions with Commentaries*. Cambridge, Mass.: Cambridge University Press, 1909.

Hughes, Everett C. "Professions." In *The Professions in America*, edited by Kenneth S. Lynn. Boston: Houghton Mifflin, 1965.

Hume, David. *Essays Moral, Political, and Literary*. 2 vols. Edited by T. H. Green and T. H. Grose. London: Longmans, 1882.

Huntington, Samuel S. *The Soldier and the State*. Cambridge, Mass.: Belknap Press of Harvard University Press, 1957.

Inlow, Gail M. *Values in Transition: A Handbook*. New York: John Wesley & Sons, 1972.

Janowitz, Morris. *The Professional Soldier: A Social and Political Portrait*. Glencoe Ill.: Free Press, 1960.

Janowitz, Morris, and Jacques van Doorn, eds. *On Military Ideology*. Rotterdam, The Netherlands: Rotterdam University Press, 1971.

Johnson, James T. *Can Modern War Be Just?* New Haven, Conn.: Yale University Press, 1984.

Johnson, James Turner. *Just War Tradition and the Restraint of War: A Moral and Historical Inquiry*. Princeton, N.J.: Princeton University Press, 1981.

Kalish, Richard A., and Kenneth W. Collier. *Exploring Human Values: Psychological and Philosophical Considerations*. Monterey, Calif.: Brooks/Cole, 1981.

Kalshoven, Frits. *The Law of Warfare*. Geneva: Henry Dunant Institute, 1973.

Kamka, Eugene, ed. *Nationalism*. Canberra: Australian National University Press, 1973.

Kant, Immanuel. In *Kant's Political Writings*, edited by Hans Reiss and translated by H. B. Nisbet. Cambridge: Cambridge University Press, 1977.

Kelley, Hugh A. *A Proposal for the United States Army Ethic*. Individual Study Project. Carlisle Barracks, Pa.: U.S. Army War College, 1984.

Kemble, Charles R. *The Image of the Army Officer in America*. Westport, Conn.: Greenwood Press, 1973.

Kriete, Charles F. "Ethical Presuppositions of the Army's Professional Slogans." *Parameters* 10 (September 1980): 86–89.

Levy, Leonard W. *Judgments: Essays on American Constitutional History*. Chicago: Quadrangle Books, 1972.

Lieberman, Jethro K. *Understanding Our Constitution*. New York: Walker, 1967.

Lillich, Richard B., and John N. Moore. *International Law Studies*. Newport, R.I.: Naval War College Press, 1980.

Lipset, Seymour. *The First New Nation*. New York: Basic Books, 1963.

Littel, Roger W. *Sociology and the Military Establishment*. New York: Russell Sage Foundation, 1965.

Locke, John. *Two Treatises of Government*. Edited by Peter Laslett. New York: New American Library, 1960.

Lynn, Kenneth S. *The Professions in America*. Boston: New American Library, 1965.

Margiotta, Franklin D., ed. *The Changing World of the American Military*. Boulder, Colo.: Westview Press, 1978.

Marqua, Francis C. *A Code of Ethics for Air Force Officers*. Individual Study Project. Maxwell Air Force Base: U.S. Air Command and Staff College, 1974.

Mavrodes, George I. "Conventions and the Morality of War." *Philosophy and Public Affairs* 4 (Winter 1980): 117–31.

McDonough, James R. *Platoon Leader*. New York: Bantam Books, 1985.

McIntyre, J. W., ed. *The Writings and Speeches of Daniel Webster*. Boston: Little, Brown & Co., 1903.

Military Ethics. Washington, D.C.: National Defense University Press, 1987.

Miller, Richard I. *The Law of War*. Lexington, Mass.: D. C. Heath, 1975.

Millett, Allan R. *Military Professionalism and Officership in America*. Columbus, Ohio: Mershon Center, 1977.

Mitchell, William C. *The American Polity*. New York: Free Press of Glencoe, 1962.

Moore, Wilbert E. *The Professions: Roles and Rules*. New York: Russell Foundation, 1976.

Murray, Richard N. *Ethics and the Army Officer: An Assessment and Recommendations for the Future*. Individual Study Project. Carlisle Barracks, Pa.: U.S. Army War College, 1984.

Narel, James L. "Values and the Professional Soldier." *Parameters* 11 (December 1981): 74–79.

Nussbaum, Arthur. *A Concise History of the Law of Nations*. New York: Macmillan, 1954.

Osgood, Robert E., and Robert W. Tucker. *Force, Order, and Justice*. Baltimore: Johns Hopkins Press, 1967.

Perry, Ralph Barton. *Realms of Value*. New York: Greenwood Press, 1968 reprint.

Pictet, Jean. *The Principles of International Humanitarian Law*. Geneva: International Committee of the Red Cross, 1966.

Potts, Robert E. *Professional Military Ethics: Are We on the Right Track?* Individual Study Project. Carlisle Barracks, Pa: U.S. Army War College, 1986.

Rawls, John. *A Theory of Justice*. Cambridge, Mass: Belknap Press of Harvard University Press, 1971.

Reese, Thomas H. "An Officer's Oath." *Military Law Review* 25 (July 1964): 1–41.

Richards, David A. J. "Reverse Discrimination and Compensatory Justice: Constitutional and Moral Theory." In *The Value of Justice*, edited by Charles A. Kelbley. New York: Fordham University Press, 1979.

Rokeach, Milton. *The Nature of Human Values*. New York: Free Press, 1973.

Rossiter, Clinton. *Seedtime of the Republic*. New York: Harcourt, Brace, 1953.

Sarkesian, Sam C. *The Professional Army Officer in a Changing Society*. Chicago: Nelson–Hall, 1975.

Schindler, Dietrich, ed. *The Laws of Armed Conflict*. Geneva: Henry Dunant Institute, 1973.

Schwander, Jeffrey L. *A Functional Army Officer Code of Ethics*. Individual Study Project. Carlisle Barracks, Pa.: U.S. Army War College, 1988.

Sherman, Edward. "Free Speech and the Military." *Update* 5 (Winter 1981): 25–27, 33–34.

Sorley, Lewis S. III. "Competence as an Ethical Imperative." *Army* 34 (August 1982): 42–48.

———. "Competence as Ethical Imperative: Issues of Professionalism." In *Military Ethics and Professionalism: A Collection of Essays*, edited by James Brown and Michael J. Collins. Washington, D.C.: National Defense University Press, 1981.

Stockholm International Peace Research Institute. *The Law of War and Dubious Weapons*. Stockholm: Almqvist & Wiksell, 1976.

Sutherland, Arthur E. *Constitutionalism in America*. New York: Blaisdell, 1965.

Taking the Stand. New York: Pocket Books, 1987. (Testimony of Oliver L. North before the Select Committee of the House and Senate)

Taylor, Maxwell D. "A Do-It-Yourself Professional Code for the Military." *Parameters* 10 (December 1980): 10–15.

Taylor, Maxwell D. "A Professional Ethic for the Military?" *Army* 28 (May 1978): 18–21.

Taylor, Robert L., and William F. Rosenbach. *Military Leadership: In Pursuit of Excellence*. Boulder, Colo.: Westview, 1984.

Taylor, Telford. *Nuremberg and Vietnam: An American Tragedy*. Chicago: Quadrangle Books, 1970.

Teichman, Jenny. *Pacifism and the Just War: A Study in Applied Philosophy*. Oxford: Basil Blackwell, 1986.

Tucker, Robert W. *The Just War*. Baltimore: Johns Hopkins Press, 1960.

Ulmer, Walter F., Jr. "The Army's New Senior Leadership Doctrine." *Parameters* 17 (December 1987): 10–17.

U.S. Air Force. *Commander's Handbook on the Law of War*, AF Pamphlet 110–34. Washington, D.C.: 1980.

———. *International Law—The Conduct of Armed Conflict and Air Operations*, AF Pamphlet 110–31. Washington, D.C.: 1976.

U.S. Army. *Fundamentals of Military Law*, ROTC Manual 145-85. Washington, D.C.: 1980.

———. *Leadership and Command at Senior Levels*, FM 22-103. Washington, D.C.: 1987.

———. *Military Leadership*, FM 22-100. Washington, D.C: 1983.

———. *Military Professionalism (Battalion Instruction)*, TC 22-9-3. Washington, D.C.: 1987.

———. *Military Professionalism (Company/Battery Instruction)*, TC 22-9-2. Washington, D.C.: 1986.

———. *Military Professionalism (Platoon and Squad Instruction)*, TC 22-9-1. Washington, D.C.: 1986.

———. *Protocols to the Geneva Conventions of 12 August 1949*, DA Pamphlet 22-1-1. Washington, D.C.: 1979.

———. *Selected Problems in the Law of War*, TC 27-10-1. Washington, D.C.: 1979.

————. *The Army*, FM 100-1. Washington, D.C.: 1986.

————. *The Law of Land Warfare*, FM 27-10. Washington, D.C.: 1956.

U.S. Army War College. *Study on Military Professionalism*. Carlisle Barracks, Pa.: U.S. Army War College, 1970.

U.S. Department of Defense. *The Armed Forces Officer*, DoD GEN-36. Washington, D.C.: GPO, 1975.

————. *Standards of Conduct*, DoD Directive 5500.7. Washington, D.C.: GPO, 1987.

U.S. Navy. *Integrity and Efficiency Training Program*, SECNAV 5370. Washington, D.C.: 1985.

————. *Standards of Conduct and Government Ethics*, SECNAV 5370.2H. Washington, D.C.: 1984.

————. *The Law of Naval Warfare*, NWIP 10–2. Washington, D.C.: 1974.

Vollmer, Howard M., and Donald L. Mills, eds. *Professionalization*. Englewood Cliffs, N.J.: Prentice Hall, 1966.

Wakin, Malham M., ed. *War, Morality, and the Military Profession*. 2d ed. Boulder, Colo.: Westview Press, 1986.

Walzer, Michael. *Just and Unjust Wars*. New York: Basic Books, 1977.

Warren, Earl. "The Bill of Rights and the Military." In *The Great Rights*, edited by Edmund Cahn. New York: Macmillan, 1963.

Wasserstrom, Richard. "Lawyers as Professionals: Some Moral Issues." *Human Rights* 5 (1975): 1–24.

Whiteman, Marjorie M. *Digest of International Law*. 15 vols. Washington, D.C.: GPO, 1968.

Williams, Robin. *American Society: A Sociological Perspective*. New York: Alfred A. Knopf, 1958.

Wolgast, Elizabeth. *The Grammar of Justice*. Ithaca, N.Y.: Cornell University Press, 1987.

Yarmolinsky, Adam. *The Military Establishment*. New York: Harper & Row, 1971.

Index